RHYTHM
of the
HEAD

Written by Georg Voros
www.georgvoros.com

All rights reserved © 2009 Georg Voros
All illustrations © 1995 Georg Voros
All illustrations Remastered Lynne Voros 2009

Cover
Lynne Voros

Published by BigDrum Publishing 2009

www.bigdrumpublishing.com

First published UK BigDrum Press 1995
©Georg Voros 1995

ISBN 978-0-620-44367-8

Other books by Georg Voros
Creating ... Performance Excellence
Fame Art Fortune
www.georgvoros.com

All Rights Reserved
No part of this publication may be reproduced, stored in a retrieval system, or transmitted in any form or means, electronic, mechanical, photocopying, recording, or otherwise without the prior written permission of the Author. This book may not be lent, re-sold, hired out or otherwise disposed of by way of trade in any form or binding or cover other than that in which it is published, without the prior consent of the Author. This book is protected by International Law which carries lawful prosecution when contravening the above.

RHYTHM of the HEAD

Georg Voros is foremost a drummer.
He has more than 35 years in the music business, has travelled extensively and is also a clinician, educator and composer.

He is the first drummer from Southern Africa to become an official Mapex drums endorsee. He also endorses Sabian cymbals and Vater drumsticks.

Georg holds two Licentiates, one in music performance and the other in teaching, both gained with distinction through Rockschool London.

Through his many years of working with top musicians, producers and engineers he brings his vast experience together creating an invaluable source of inspirational information for drummers of all levels, age and gender.

Read more about Georg on his website at www.georgvoros.com

ACKNOWLEDGEMENTS

I would like to thank all the incredible drummers and teachers who took the time to read and endorse this book. I am very flattered and deeply indebted. Thanks to Carl Palmer, Lloyd Ryan, Virgil Donati, Gary Husband, Peter Baron, Steve White, Bill Bruford, Mark Mondesir, Francis Seriau.

Special thanks to Global Drumming Ambassador Dom Famularo, who took time out of his famously busy schedule to honor me with his Foreword for this revised edition and also for his friendship, support and invaluable advice over the years.

To all those drummers who read the first edition – thank you for your kind words, praise and support. You were the inspiration for me writing this edition.

And thanks also to my wife Lynne for all her effort and work on this new book.

This book is dedicated to my family, I thank you for your love and support. You guys are the best and I love you big time.

Dedication to Jim Chapin

Just before we went to print I heard the sad news of Jim Chapin's passing. I was one of the fortunate many to have been personally touched by the 'Chapin magic' when Jim introduced me to the Moeller technique many years ago. Jim was charming and I loved his wit and enthusiasm for life and drumming, and on the occasions we were together I felt privileged to come into contact with one of drummings legends – which of course I had. Jim lived a long full life and I am extremely grateful to have been a very small part of it.

RIP Jim, your legend continues...

Chapter		Page
	Preface	7
	Foreword by Dom Famularo	9
	Introduction	11
1	getting things into perspective	17
2	it takes time	24
3	ESP – extra slow playing	32
4	no pain no gain?	39
5	is setting goals relevant to achieving success?	43
6	using other drummers as role models	52
7	how to keep on being enthusiastic	56
8	money or art?	64
9	how to deal effectively with criticism	69
10	positive attitude – do you have it?	75
11	how to compete by not being competitive	82
12	how to develop a good reputation	87
13	how to make the most of your full potential	91
14	how to increase your powers of observation and listening	94
15	practising and playing to recorded music	100
16	drummers are real musicians	106
17	how to successfully prepare for auditions	114
18	working with established names and celebrities	122
19	how to achieve your best onstage drum mix	128
20	how to be creative in any musical situation	133
21	the overplaying factor	137
22	demo packages – making them work for you	142
23	drumming and your health	151
24	your personal global agency – the internet	162
25	creative visualization – a powerful process!	169
26	don't hide your light under a drum set	176
	Glossary	183
	Further recommended reading	185

Preface

Welcome to this newly revised and up to date edition of *Rhythm of the Head*.

Many years have passed since this book was originally published in 1995. I am immensely proud of this work. What was initially a wild idea, putting some thoughts and ideas to paper, just to see what might happen, has proven to be quite a personal triumph! Little did I realize how this book would affect and influence so many people. If you had told me that it would form the basis of school and college projects, be quoted in university theses, or change practice and performance attitudes, I would have seriously questioned your foresight.

In the original edition of *Rhythm of the Head*, I didn't re-invent the wheel in offering never-before-heard-of motivational information; I merely took existing thoughts and ideas and turned them into my own by using real-life and career experiences. Also, many drummers who have read the first book and with whom I was fortunate to have personal contact, remarked on how easy it was to read and how much common sense it contained. The kind of common sense where you might think, "I know that, so why don't I use it?" Or "why didn't I think of that?"

That was it! The primary aim of the book was to get the information across in a simple and easy to understand format. Many times drummers would tell me that they managed to read *Rhythm of the Head* in one or two days. One drummer I met told me that he read the book five times while on holiday with his folks! I don't take comments like this lightly and I thank each and every person who read the first edition.

So, why not a *Rhythm of the Head* Part 2, as many drummers requested? I personally didn't think a sequel was the way to go, as the original book contained the key elements and most important information I wanted to share. I was also fearful of putting out a sequel that didn't measure up to the first book. I find it rare that a sequel is equal to, or better than its predecessor. Out of this viewpoint came the idea of producing a revised edition – the same book, but more up to date and containing additional newer information. The world in 2009 is now quite different to what it was in 1995 when this book first emerged. The internet was no-where to be seen and music and recording technology has evolved greatly since that time. Also, many drummers reading this revised edition will have been in kindergarten or junior school when the original came out and possibly missed it. It is in regard to this newer generation of drummers that this book has been modernized. I also believe (not because it has more information to impart), that this new edition is a better book. It is better because the writing has come of age and I feel that I possess more in-depth knowledge now in what I do, as opposed to where I was in 1995.

Finally, just as I did many years ago when writing this book in taking existing ideas and concepts and turning them into my own, so too should you do the same with the information I offer in this book. Take the ideas and concepts offered here and integrate them into your personal situation and make them work for you – in your own way.

I hope you enjoy reading this 21st century edition of *Rhythm of the Head* as much as I enjoyed writing it.

Georg Voros – 2009

Foreword

"I travel the world playing/teaching/writing and studying drums. I had the opportunity, many years ago, to meet Georg in the UK and then again in South Africa. We performed together many times and taught many drummers in these tours.

I am so impressed with Georg as a player/teacher/musician/writer and his dedication to research, in this book, the ultimate journey we face as musicians...how we can prepare our mind, our attitude and our destiny! *Rhythm of the Head* is the guide to understanding the obstacles we will encounter in the music industry.

We use a small percentage of our brain limiting our potential for greater results. Socrates said...'An unexamined life is not worth living.' To question ourselves and be willing to grow and change is the true path to success. It may take some reprogramming of old bad habits to evolve them into new good habits!

To pursue new mental techniques and open doors of achievement is a proven way to tap into unused potential! As there are rudiments in drumming....this is a fundamental rudiment of life!

I especially like the new added chapters....'Creative Visualization' which is a technique I continue to use in my global travels, 'Your Personal Global Agency - The Internet' which offers the understanding of you getting your message to the globe from your computer! 'How to achieve your best onstage drum mix' also helps greatly with getting the most results from your sound!

Einstein said, 'You cannot solve new challenges with old

solutions.' What Georg has given us is are tools for new solutions! Read carefully and apply these ideas into your daily life of being a musician in today's world! Build the career you want!

Each of us walks and lives life to the beat of a different drummer. Some people make waves...some people ride the wave and others spend their entire life looking for the beach! You must decide where you fit in and where you want to be!

We learn the rhythm of drumming to give us the vocabulary to express ourselves in any musical situation. Now is the time to learn the *Rhythm of the Head* to give us the chance to move forward in our desire to share our talent with the world!

Be the wave maker and enjoy each word you read....!"

Dom Famularo
Drumming's Global Ambassador

Introduction

In the beginning there was a drum ... it followed that a drummer was born and he played the drum ... from that drum evolved the drum set. Drums, in all shapes, sizes and sounds have been around for centuries. It is a fact that the 'drum' was the first 'musical' instrument ever known.

In the early part of the 20th century the set of drums was formally named and they called it the 'traps' – deriving from the word contraption. These early traps consisted of a snare drum and large military type bass drum (both covered in calf skin drum heads), augmented by all manner of contraptions such as temple blocks, cymbals, cow bells, triangles and other percussion of the day.

And so it was that there came many drummers and with them the drum set developed – right up to the present time, where the sophistication and innovation of the drummer's tools is indeed staggering.

We have computer designed (CAD/CAM) drum heads, we are offered a multitude of drum finishes ranging from standard factory finish to chic custom designs. Drum shells with flawlessly correct bearing edges are constructed from birch, maple, mahogany, merranti and many other woods to shape our desired sound. Hardware is available in every weight and size catering to the most demanding needs and wants of every style of drummer. Digital drums give us a world of computerized sounds at our fingertips in the form of pads, triggers and samples. Cymbals are works of art, painstakingly hammered out by both master craftsmen and state of the art machinery. Yes, we have it all.

Drums and drumming is BIG business with many followers and practitioners of this age-old art.

And ever since those early days of the traps, drum instruction material has appeared in all manner and form: from stylized books dealing in one genre of music such as rock, jazz, funk, Latin, military etc, to method books that test our endurance, coordination, control and concentration. There are also self-contained drum courses in audio and DVD formats teaching beats and fills with the essential rudiments thrown in. For all drummers, whatever their standard of playing, this study material serves an important purpose in that it is essential for continuing musical growth – on a practical level.

But what about the other side? The hidden element that cannot be seen or touched? The <u>mental process</u> that occurs when you are practicing or performing, or even when you are simply thinking about what you want to play and how to <u>play better</u>.

For example:
• how do you maintain enthusiasm in the face of setbacks?
• why do drummers with lesser ability sometimes do better than those with superior ability?
• is setting goals an integral part on your road to success?
• if so how do you define success?
• are you an eternal 'bedroom musician'?
• how valid is the age-old adage 'no pain no gain' in your practice?

These questions and many more are dealt with and answered in the following pages of this book.

Rhythm of the Head is not intended to teach you how to play the drums. No, the previously mentioned instructional materials will take care of that. Rather this book is all about <u>attitude</u>! The correct attitude needed to develop your <u>full potential</u> and get the most out of <u>your</u> drumming in the <u>best</u> possible way.

Each and every one of us is an individual in both playing and personality and what one drummer might need to improve his or her playing, won't apply to all drummers. This aside, ALL drummers from beginner to professional and regardless of whatever style of music they play, require certain correct knowledge and information to get the job done properly. Naturally gifted players do of course have an advantage, but all the talent in the world will do them precious little good if they don't know how to correctly channel this in order to play at their peak level of performance, and also are not able to work with others on both a harmonious musical and social level.

This book may also be regarded as a manual or reference, containing keys to open up your mind and playing, enabling you to accomplish your musical goals. I believe that aside from poor technique, two of the biggest barriers for any musician in obtaining and achieving optimum performance in their playing is due to mental blocks and/or incorrect thinking. No matter how good your practical skills, if your mind is filled with negative, self-limiting thoughts, then this can only lead to one result – a bad performance.

Rhythm of the Head is a book for <u>all drummers</u>! It is the result of over thirty years music industry experience in my roles of drummer, educator, clinician and author. The contents are based upon research by interaction with other musicians though performing, talking, experimenting, teaching, listening, studying, debating, learning, practicing, making mistakes, recording and virtually all other areas of the business. It is also reinforced with other successful drummers' ideas, beliefs, experiences and comments on the subject.

The information contained within these pages is aimed at encouraging you to be the best drummer you can possibly become.

Ready to get started on this great learning curve? Here we go...

If a man does not keep pace with his companions

Perhaps it is because he hears a different drummer

Let him step to the music he hears

However measured or far away

Thoreau

getting things into perspective

So if you hadn't heard of me before buying this book, you might think, "okay, he makes sense and all this sounds cool, but just who is this Georg Voros character? "

Fair observation, after all I'm not exactly a household name like Travis Barker, Tommy Lee, Charlie Watts, or others of the same stature. Perhaps your curiosity was aroused by the fact that here you have a book written by an 'unknown' (all things being relative) drummer, endorsed and recommended by drummers whom you have heard of? How is this possible? Am I not supposed to be a 'famous name' drummer myself in order to have got this book to that point?

Well, at this stage I won't divulge how and why this all came about, but it's safe to say that the techniques and information covered in this book helped me to get it into the position that I finally wanted it to rest, and that is in your hands!

fame and fortune

You see what I represent is a whole lot more important than who I am – and without sounding self-important or vain, you could say that I represent 95% of the drumming community. Yep, I see your eyebrows rising and you're thinking "why"? Well, here's why ...

Like it or not the truth of the matter is that only a small percentage of drummers go on to achieve the dizzy heights of international stardom and fame. But within the same breath I also add and firmly believe that you can't keep a good man (or girl) down forever. Let me make this point... Of the huge majority of drummers who never *make it*, a large number do have flits with stardom and the big time, and may have stayed there had they been better prepared. So let's now get a clearer perspective on this whole stardom thing.

What one musician considers doing well or having *cracked it* another may not. Okay, so the most obvious and ultimate level of success for most would be jetting around the world with a chart busting band, playing to sell-out arena audiences, staying in the best hotels, having a large road crew to carry and set up the gear, fighting off (or maybe not) the groupies trying to break through the backstage door and then, finally, arriving home to your mansion with your beloved Porsche patiently waiting in the garage. Right? Does this sound like a dream to you? To most it is – but to a few it isn't. If you consider the famous quote: "anything is possible to a willing mind", why is it that only a small percentage ever reach these spectacular heights? What's more perplexing is that many of the musicians who do manage to attain this level may not even be considered very good players. Hmmm... what is it with this stardom thing then, what about the bulk of the players, the 95% who don't get there – the 'unknowns'? They're everywhere! Their faces are on posters in your town or city – you read about them in your local and national press – music stores love them because they're the lifeblood keeping them solvent. You listen and see them playing at your local bar and club or even concert halls – you hear them being played on your local and national radio stations – you may even see them on TV – many travel and see the world for FREE. Yes, they are indeed everywhere and getting paid for doing what they love to do – play music. Some are better known and better paid than others and this is where the personal perspective on the success factor comes into play. This is because I've known 'infamous' Top 40 club musicians who have their big houses, big pools, big cars and on weekends might go hang gliding, sailing or even clock up their flying hours to obtain a pilots license – whatever!

A personal profile

If I may now digress slightly, I'd like to illustrate briefly what an 'unknown' (again all things being relative) drummer can and has accomplished – ME.

In South Africa:
- I've played in two bands that had number one chart hits

- Played on an international Worldvision release – along the same lines as the UK's 'Feed the World' Band Aid single
- Worked with local and international artists on tour and in the studio.
- Recorded drums and percussion for the stage show aired at the 2003 World Parks Summit attended by ex-president Nelson Mandela
- Founded South Africa's first magazine for drummers (sold in 2006)
- Undertook the first South African double clinic tour with Global Drum Ambassador Dom Famularo
- Played major drum events with drummers such as Jojo Mayer and Marco Minnemann

Internationally:
- I've worked for a UK soul artist who has had hits released in many countries
- I've been a member of a band signed to a major American publishing company and record label
- Recorded an album with a band nominated for the Mercury Music 'Best Album of the Year'
- Played with a band which won the (BCMA) 'Best country band' award four times! I was in the band when we won it for the third time.
- With the same band I recorded an album play listed on CMTV Europe, appearing in countries as far afield as Russia
- I'm listed in two music Encyclopedia's (American and South African), which means I've managed to get my name into print... forever
- I've recorded in state of the art studios with top engineers and producers
- I've signed autographs and had my photo taken by fans and journalists
- Done a record album cover shoot in famous pop and rock photographer David Bailey's studio in London (the Rolling Stones had been in the week before – and then the week after our shoot The Who were there)
- I've appeared in pop/rock/country music magazines and national newspapers
- I've wined and dined on a record company's expense account – funny how food always tastes better that way
- I've had the opportunity of traveling to and working in many countries around the world

- I've performed live in various settings from small clubs, theaters to stadiums
- I have a strong global Internet presence – Don't take me word for it, Google my name and check it out!
- I have drum, cymbal, head and stick endorsements
- And then, of course I have this book which is endorsed by drummers like Virgil Donati, Bill Bruford and Carl Palmer – not because they were paid to do it, but on the strength of the content. Not to forget the Foreword kindly contributed by Dom Famularo!

5% or 95% – that is the question

So where do you think this list belongs. In the 5% or the 95% category? Personally I like to think it's a bit of both. I accept that it's not quite on the same level as touring with a mega outfit such as 'U2', but hey, I've had a good time and I still am, earning my living from what I love and do best – playing music. And now also teaching, writing and presenting clinics. As the great actor George Burns once said, "the secret to long life and happiness is to like what you do for a living". I couldn't agree more. You know it's a sad fact that around 17% of people on this planet hate what they do for a living. Hey, I think that's tragic don't you think? I can honestly say that when I get up in the morning I look forward to the day because I am working in the field that I have chosen. If you're not currently doing this then I truly hope that you take on board the information presented in this book as this will help you achieve what you want – but my disclaimer is... only if you work at it!

A lot of people would sell their grandmothers to achieve what I've outlined above in my list of accomplishments. I know this for a fact because they've told me so! But I'm not unique in this as there are many drummers out there who have had comparable success and more – yet they are still the *unknowns*. You see it's difficult to sometimes define the line separating the 95% and the 5%, but in the end I have to say that it's really down to your own interpretation and ideals. I've met some pretty successful drummers who are rather humble regarding their achievements and don't think it's such a big deal.

no hard fast rules

As you advance further into this book you may find

that some chapters seem to overlap each other in content and ideas. Since this is normally the case in real life why not then in drumming?

Consider this. A paradiddle is a rudiment made up of eight notes – the sticking being RLRR LRLL. Right? Now start by breaking down this group of eight into two halves and you find yourself with one group of four notes being RLRR, and the other group of four being LRLL. Halve each of these two four note groups and you find yourself with (a) two separate single stroke groups – one being RL and the other LR, and (b) the other two halves are double note groups made up of RR and LL respectively. Go even further and halve these two doubles groups and they give you (a) one group of two single strokes R and R, and (b) the other group with two L and L single strokes.

Now, after all this subdivision, look at the figure below and ask yourself is a paradiddle:

(a) made up of one group of eight notes;

(b) two separate groups containing singles and doubles in each;

(c) four groups comprising two groups of doubles and two groups of singles;

OR

(d) eight single notes?

Confused?

Read it again and when you understand and come to your decision, you'll find that once again it's down to your own interpretation. All answers are in essence correct because they all lead to the same result. The secret is in how you internalize it.

The Paradiddle
1) RLRRLRLL   – One group of eight
2) RLRR LRLL   – Two groups of four
3) RL RR LR LL   – Four groups of two
4) R L R R L R L L   – Eight singles

To many drummers the above example may seem quite self evident, but to the novice (and even some more experienced players), it may have opened up a new way of approaching not just rudiments, but drumming in general.

to sum up

So as illustrated in the practical side of drumming where

ideas and content overlap, so too does this occur in the hidden *mental side*. And the more you read into this book you may find yourself disagreeing with certain philosophies and ideas presented. Good! Because it will show that this book is achieving what I wanted it to achieve – for you to deeply <u>think</u> about and <u>challenge</u> what you want to accomplish by devising your own personal route in order to successfully realize those goals – and if anything I suggest is wholly or even partly responsible for your success, then we've both achieved our goals.

    Good luck!

it takes time

One of the first things to realize when wanting to play any musical instrument in an accomplished manner is that there are no shortcuts to achieving this goal. To attain even a reasonable amount of competence requires a certain amount of dedicated time and effort – after all, anything worthwhile takes some degree of self-sacrifice. But by self-sacrifice I don't mean that you have to put yourself through hell in order to achieve your aims. No, practicing is a great challenge and need not be sterile and boring. It's all down to the way in which you approach it.

professors of music

I remember back to my first year of high school. I'd been playing drums for a couple of years and had my own three-piece rock band that was doing mainly informal (unpaid) gigs for friends. We had also managed at that early stage to do a few *real* club dates – so being young and very keen we always had lots to talk about regarding music.

One day, in a break between classes, a guitarist friend and I were discussing music in general and the technicalities of playing our respective instruments. A non-musician classmate listening in on our conversation decided to add his five cents worth and exclaimed:

"Listen Voros, all you need to play drums, is be fast".

"Oh yeah?" I replied, "what about beats and rudiments and..."

"Na", he interrupted, "you just have to be fast".

I never forgot this encounter and it was at the tender age of 13 that I was first introduced to other people's misconceptions of what it takes to play drums and be a drummer. I prepared myself, because I knew then that I would have many more encounters with these *experts* on the instrument.

Now to be fair and in defense (but not much) of these self-acclaimed *professors of music*, I can see why they say what they say. Quite simply, when watching and listening to a good drummer in action, what they witness is a relaxed and seemingly effortless flow of rhythms, making it look easy. The *prof* may even be fooled into thinking that this skilled exponent of the drums isn't really trying that hard. But little does our *shmu...expert* realize that in order to reach such a standard of musicianship; the accomplished drummer will have spent countless hours engaged in practice and performance situations.

He will have experimented with ideas, tried new concepts, played with numerous musicians of all caliber, changed drum set-ups many times, continually questioned his playing and generally involved himself in a myriad of activities to perfect his drumming. In short, he will have honed all his skills to the point that what would be on show would be the culmination of many years of dedicated practice, study and performance.

What's your reason?

When a student starts studying drums, he or she will have their own specific reason(s) for wanting to take up the instrument. Some examples I've heard from students in my teaching studio are:
- I just want to play for fun
- I want to make it to the top
- I want to be a session player
- My time sucks
- My band have suggested that I take some lessons to improve my technique
- It's something I've always wanted to do but never got round to doing
- I want to earn a living from music
- I lack confidence in my playing
... and so on and so on.

As a teacher, I am respectful of any and all reasons to take up playing the drums as they are personal and valid to the individuals concerned. Also, I don't concern myself too much with a reason that at first might seem unrealistic. This is because once a student makes some headway into tuition and playing, he or she starts to gain a clearer perspective and understanding on drumming and what will be required in order to achieve their chosen goal or goals.

give it time

This may happen when, having embarked on a course of drum study, a student finds that it all starts to happen very quickly and a bit too easily. Drumming can be like this as a reasonable amount of competence can be gained in a relatively short space of time. However this competence is usually only in the basics: a few rhythms, some fills, and maybe the easier rudiments thrown in. Once more complex and demanding study is attempted, the learning curve then starts to level out dramatically and the rate of accomplishment slows down considerably. Typical scenarios of this may look something like this...

Scenario #1 Armed with a few basics, the student decides he's had enough of lessons and is now ready to do it. Not realizing just what he has let himself in for, he ventures out and in a relatively short space of time falls flat on his face. This results in him soon losing confidence in his playing. This could be because he joined a band way out of his league and found that he just couldn't stand the pace and keep up with the other more experienced musicians. Disillusioned he leaves, or even worse, is 'asked' to leave. At this point he either sells his drums or if made of sterner stuff, decides to accept the challenge and seek out how and why he went wrong by going back to his drum teacher, or starting a disciplined path of self-instruction.

Scenario #2 Maybe the student didn't even join a band but decided to completely go it alone by pursuing a course of self-study, only to hit a stone wall by not knowing which way to go to advance due to a lack of experience and knowledge.

Does this sound like a contradiction? Read on...

These two scenarios are basically negative examples, but have worked out for some drummers.

Never fortunate enough to have a private teacher or formal college study, I took it upon myself to undergo the self-study route. I suppose that some would have described my enthusiasm in my early teens as obsessive. I used to eat, drink and sleep drums, practicing for hours and hours on end. On Saturday nights while my buddies were in the back row of the movies making out, I would be at home working on my flamadiddle. Was this normal? Well, it was for me at the time.

I look back on all of this with fond affection and a sense of self-admiration, but at the same time realize that I would have advanced a whole lot quicker if I had had the fortune of a guiding hand. I blindly stumbled through my formative playing years hungrily grabbing and taking whatever advice (good or bad) that came my way. Fortunately for me this worked out and was a good thing as it gave me a strong sense of self-independence and discipline, allowing me to develop at my own pace without any outside pressure. By the time I was 16 and in my first semi-professional residency gig, I was used to thinking and sorting things out for myself, and whatever skills and knowledge I lacked to get the job done, I duly corrected. I regard this as an essential and extremely useful trait for anyone entering this tough music business.

So while for me the self-study route worked to a larger extent, this may not be the case for all students. Self-study requires immense self-discipline and you need strong determination to succeed.

consistency yields the best results

If you have limited time for practice then it is better to put in half an hour a day, than skip your practice sessions for three or four days and then *make it up* by sitting down for four hours.

Consistent every day practice yields the best results. You establish a momentum by giving your drumming a sense of continuity and flow, as your mental and physical muscles are always *flexed* and ready for action. Additionally, through continuous practice (and performance) you keep yourself abreast of the ever-changing developments in the world of drums and drumming, staying alert to any fresh opportunities that may come your way – and seizing them!

the time is there

The older we get the more responsibilities we have to face up to – this is a basic fact of life. Those of you who put in a full days work with only some evenings and the weekend to devote to practice and performing will agree that it gets harder to find the time. Even with the best of intentions, if you don't put in the required time and effort for practice, you won't gain a lot of ground.

The secret here is to make the most of your available time! Grab that practice pad and put in some time while you break for lunch – use the time on the bus or train to study new material – instead of watching that TV program that you just *can't afford to miss* get some essential practice in – if you have a social commitment that you don't really need (or want) to attend then cancel it and use the time for yourself – let your buddy drive while you practice your double paradiddle... the time is there if you look for it and are really serious about improving.

If you're concerned about the *noise factor* that may offend the neighbors, then put your thinking cap on. Use a practice pad kit or if you can afford one, get an electronic kit. If the idea of none of those appeals to you then check out those silencer pads that fit onto acoustic drum sets. They're a reasonably cheap option to ensure that you keep practicing. Hey, I know nothing beats playing on a well-tuned acoustic set-up but if noise constraints kick in then go for second best, whatever that is.

Here's a cool example in how one of my ingenious drum students got around the noise factor. He built what he called a *practice box* in his attic! He used the term box, because he built *a box within a box*, which is really the best way of soundproofing. He lined the walls and ceiling with a sound insulating absorbent material known in the UK as Rock wool. This is a relatively cheap material and you can liken this to the material used as underlay for floor carpeting. In fact you can use whatever sound absorbing material you can lay your hands on – as long as it's dense and can soak up sound waves. He then covered this material with sheets of cheap chipboard wood. Finally, he dampened the sound even further by covering the wood with old carpet. The end result: effective and inexpensive sound dampening. He had devised a means and place where he could practice uninterrupted.

Where there's a will there's a way and if you're keen enough you will find the way.

plan ahead

If you pride yourself on the fact that you religiously practice four to six hours a day, I admire your dedication. But if all you're doing during your practice sessions is aimlessly repeating over and over what you can already play comfortably, then have a re-think. You might not be getting as much out of your practice as another drummer who spends only one or two hours a day constantly challenging himself by stretching his abilities and always striving to learn new material.

Unfamiliar territory is not always comfortable and it is a human trait to want to bask in the warmth of comfortable surroundings. For us musicians, these surroundings represent knowledge. Get a balance between focusing on the *comfortable* and the *uncomfortable* areas of your drumming. The comfortable side keeps alive your enthusiasm for playing by constantly boosting and pumping your *ego* with what you already do well. And by striving to learn new unfamiliar material, you won't get bored and lose your desire to improve and play the drums.

In reality, most drummers do seem to achieve a comfortable blend of the two. If you have not, then seriously consider the above and *practice smart*.

Play it over and over

In order to achieve a relaxed and comfortable feel in your playing, many repetitions of your chosen drum exercises and material will be required.

Consider this: When you undertake to learn a new motor skill (which is basically anything requiring repetitive practice), a lot of conscious thought is applied. Good examples would be attempting to drive a car or ride a bicycle. At first every little movement and action is performed with a tremendous amount of conscious thought and effort – you really have to think about what you're doing. All of a sudden you hit on the right way of doing what's required and click(!), the brain registers this as being correct. You repeat the same action and eventually, after many repetitions, it becomes permanently stamped on your memory. The action is now spontaneously executed and no longer needs extreme conscious thought. You may even wonder why you had so much difficulty getting started in the first place.

Now apply this principle to the drums and this is what happens: After spending the necessary time engaged in repetitions of your chosen drum material, you'll discover that your drumming (execution) starts to shift from conscious (thinking) playing to unconscious (non-thinking) playing. It is now taking on a more natural and spontaneous form. What this means is that instead of concentrating all of your efforts on what you're physically playing at the time, your concentration centers more on the music you're playing. Your drumming takes care of itself because you are confident in your ability. You know that you've put in the required practice to handle the situation in hand. You're now on the road to becoming a much more musical drummer rather than one who just bangs out a beat. However, this desired result takes time and can only come about after constant repetition of the correct action(s) required. Don't kid yourself; there is no shortcut to achieving this.

To sum up

Most individuals have definite ideas on what and where they want to be in the drumming world, whereas some may not be very specific. Try and get some perspective on why you're playing or want to play the drums. If you want to play for fun and just jam with friends on the weekend then cool, you won't have to handle too much pressure. If, on the other hand, your aim is to make it to the top of the session world, then realize that a whole lot more dedication and effort is going to be required.

These two examples scream out common sense, but I've given them anyway because I still meet people who are pretty naïve about what is required of them, and also how long it will take for them to achieve what they desire.

Lastly, whatever you decide remember to always keep an open mind and not approach your drumming with too many conditions. Be a sponge and soak up as much information as you can. And the further you advance into your playing the better you will be able to decide what is needed in order for your personal development... and what is not.

ESP – extra slow playing

Some drummers are of the opinion that practicing at a slow pace is reserved only for beginners and the incompetent, and that being able to play very fast is the sign of an accomplished player. The latter statement is partly true, but the first is false and quickly changes as soon as extra slow playing is attempted.

microscopic drumming

In my teaching studio I've seen experienced drummers turn red with embarrassment when, at my request, they've slowed down their playing only to find out just how imprecise whatever they are attempting to play really is.

For example: when a double stroke roll is played at 160bpm (beat per minute), then slowed down to a tempo of 60bpm, all kinds of evils are revealed in its execution, pinpointing why the rudiment in question is not happening the way it should. Any drummer worth their salt will agree that it is harder to keep steady time combined with good feel at a slow tempo, than a quick pace. Oh yes, keeping a ballad solid with an in the pocket backbeat requires a whole lot more concentration than an uptempo rhythm.

By slowing down your playing, you make it possible to listen closely to every note being played. You have the opportunity to feel if there is tension present in any part of your body and duly eliminate it. Incorrect hand and feet movement can be checked and corrected by the use of a mirror. Attempting to read an exercise or piece of music is made infinitely easier by slowing down the tempo, so you can take in every note and rest on the page. In essence what you are doing with ESP is putting your drumming under a microscope and getting to the root cause – by smoothing out and refining all aspects of your performance.

On the Pulse

I first started thinking about Extra Slow Playing when I read an article featuring a well known drummer who, at the time, was a member of a hugely successful American rock band. He said that when starting out he would practice his technical and rudimental exercises in an open to close to open manner – this means practicing from slow to fast then back to slow, therefore not playing them in strict tempo. As a result of this practice method, he found that when attempting to lay down solid straight time with a band, his timing was all over the place. Alarmed at what was happening he set out to put this right by spending the next few months at Berklee College in Boston. His drum tutor instructed him to work through material from the George L. Stone book 'Stick Control' (one of the drumming bibles!). The stipulation was that all exercises had to be played in strict time to a metronome and at extremely slow tempos – between 40 to 80bpm. The object of this discipline? To force him to listen closely to the metronomic pulse and attempt to play exactly with and on the time, being laid down.

Now, if you've never tried this and think it sounds easy, I urge you to give it a go. You don't even have to use the 'Stick Control' book or any other book, just play some single and double strokes. You'll be surprised at how difficult this can be. Put down this book, grab your sticks and turn on your metronome to 40bpm and play. Go on, do it now. Remember, the object of the exercise is to play precisely on the beat, and you know you're doing it right when you can't hear the metronome.

Well, how was it? Did you start off all over the place and get it together the more you played? Did you find yourself in the pocket at times? And, when you realized you were, did you find yourself slipping out of time? Were you aware of any flamming taking place between your strokes and the click? No matter how well or bad you did, realize that Extra Slow Playing is an ongoing discipline and once integrated into your practice routine, will be of invaluable use irrespective of whatever level of drummer you aspire to be... and become.

expanding the concept

This practice method can be applied to all areas of drumming. For snare drum use I suggest starting off with your leading hand and playing just single notes. Strive to play precisely on each click emitted by the metronome. In the silent spaces between the clicks, get used to singing and feeling the subdivided notes. For example: if you're subdividing an eighth note rhythm in 4/4 time, then you'll be physically playing on all the numbers (1234 – which are the quarter note counts), and singing between these on the eighth note (an) counts. Therefore: 1 (an) 2 (an) 3 (an) 4 (an). Should you be subdividing in triplets, as in 12/8 time, then again you'll be playing on all the numbers (1234 – quarter note counts), and singing on the an ah's. Therefore: 1 (an ah) 2 (an ah) 3 (an ah) 4 (an ah). The same applies to sixteenth note rhythms. Once you can confidently sing and feel these subdivisions between the quarter note counts, then physically play them. Lastly, use rudiments, reading exercises and any other study material that you can apply to snare drum practice and listen and watch closely.

For drum set study, try dissecting your rhythms! Let's start with a very simple exercise: With your metronome set between 40 and 60bpm, start playing quarter notes on your hihat and keep this up for around three to four minutes. When you feel it's in the pocket, then add your other hand on beats two and four on snare drum, making sure that the limb playing the hihat retains the original relaxed feel. Play these two for another few minutes and then add your bass drum, making sure that the feel between your two hands does not change in sound or physical sensation. Is your foot relaxed? Should you wish to incorporate all four limbs then start off the exercise with your leading hand on your ride cymbal or remote hihat and go through the process as described above and then add in your left foot by pedaling on hihat. Left handed players will of course reverse this process.

You can also start off with any limb and add the other limbs in any order to make it more interesting and challenging. The better you become at this exercise, the more aware you'll become of the endless variations that you can work with. For example: aside from just quarter notes on the hihat you could use eighth notes, triplet feels such as shuffles, sixteenth note rhythms incorporating one or both hands and so on – hey, the possibilities are endless, so be creative!

There have been times when I've used this method of

practice, and got so into the pocket with the click that I've stopped to check whether it was still on and working. It's a good feeling when this happens, because you know you're doing it right and are moving ahead.

it pays off

My first studio session with a click was not a very enjoyable experience; in short I screwed up... and screwed up badly! Drum machines had been on the market a couple of years with the "Linn" in particular creating huge paranoia amongst drummers the world over. Good solid time was demanded more than ever from real drummers because if they couldn't cut it, a machine would replace them!

My nightmare session occurred when the producer requested I play along to a click because the time was wandering. Being the first time I had ever done this in a studio, I was totally unprepared and did a poor job. As a result I was relieved of my duties – that's right I got fired! Needless to say, this painful experience badly affected my confidence, but after a short time I picked myself up and resolved to correct this thorn in my side – engaging in intensive (and extensive) Extra Slow Playing always to a metronome.

I pulled my rudimental and snare drum playing apart. I stripped down my beats in the manner described earlier, striving to 'become one' with the click. Additionally, to ensure that my subdivision of notes was as accurate and evenly spaced as I could play them, I indulged in the following: if, for example, I was playing a groove with a quarter note rhythm on the hihat, I would sing eighth note, triplet and sixteenth note hihat subdivisions while still only physically playing the quarter notes. I took this further with what I call polyrhythmic singing. For example, when playing a sixteenth note hihat pattern I'd sing a triplet rhythm against it, or when playing a triplet hihat pattern I'd sing an eighth note rhythm and so on.

I also engaged in a practice I call 'mind drums'. This is where I sit with the metronome switched on and clicking away, imagining (seeing and hearing) myself playing along perfectly in time. In other words Creative Visualization, which is covered in greater detail in chapter 24. You can do this while sitting at your drum set imagining yourself playing, or anywhere by just closing your eyes and seeing your setup in front of you. If this sounds a bit weird to you then let me assure you that it does work. I believe that before you can transfer anything down to your limbs, you have to be able either to hear it in your head, sing it, or see it in your mind. Once you start to utilize these techniques, things will come to you a lot quicker.

So as you see from the above, it was my turn to put my drumming under the microscope... and it paid off a few years later.

While in London, one of the signed bands I was involved with was recording their first album. It was my first big international session and therefore obviously very important to me. The recording engineer, having worked with top drummers such as Steve Ferrone and Mike Baird, knew his business and what he was talking about. He made all my metronomic Extra Slow Playing practice worthwhile.

I had finished laying down my tracks and we were taking a short break. Discussing the recording, we got into the subject of my freshly recorded drum tracks. I asked him what he thought of my playing and in particular how I did when playing to click. He complimented me by saying that I worked quickly and was very good playing to click. Phew! After my disastrous entry into the world of playing along to click, those few words were music to my ears (excuse the pun!). All those hours spent working in Extra Slow Playing had been more than worth it! The result is that I'm happy with the job I did on the album and on listening back am pleased with what is coming back at me from the speakers.

Before closing this chapter, I'd like to share with you another worthwhile, but quite different result from engaging in ESP practice. It occurred one night while playing with an original funk/rock band. All the keyboard and bass lines were being run from a sequencer, which basically means I was playing along to a machine in a live situation. I suppose really that I could afford to be a bit off the mark here and there as the clinical perfection required in a studio environment did not exist. Nonetheless, it was still my intention to be tight with the click, but to also make the music groove by not sounding like I was playing to a machine.

A keyboard player (*see footnote) who was on a UK tour with a rock revue show, happened to be in the venue on this particular night. During our break he approached me and we talked. He complimented me by saying that I sounded very natural playing to the click and it did not sound like I was being restricted by the bleep in my headphones. Now, I know from experience and talking to other drummers that many are not comfortable using a click in live situation, saying that it restricts their natural flow and feel. In most cases I think this is due not to a lack of ability, but more so to insufficient time spent practicing and performing in this manner.

ongoing benefits

Even now, after many years of playing, whenever I feel uncomfortable with my drumming for whatever reason, I indulge in some Extra Slow Playing. I find that this discipline dissolves any anxieties, relaxes overly tense muscles, sharpens up my focus and generally centers my playing.

to sum up

By using and sticking to the ESP method, you will reap the benefits. It will cause your drumming to become tight with and without a click. Your articulation will be cleaner and more precise; you will develop more control in the physical execution demanded from all four of your limbs; your feel will improve by your gaining a better understanding of why whatever you're playing sounds the way it is.

Extra Slow Playing is for all drummers regardless of their skill level.

*Footnote: As a result of the keyboard player liking the way I played that night, he later offered me work with the same rock revue show – which I duly took up!

no pain no gain?

This whole chapter could be summed up in two words – BE SENSIBLE.

I remember back to when I was younger and I would set myself grueling practice sessions. One of the reasons being that I could then boast to my friends by proudly announcing, "oh yeah, I practice six hours a day, no matter what"... and wait for their impressed response. Their answers would usually be something like, "wow this guy is really into it, what dedication".

Although this was true, I was dedicated all right, and I still am, only now my practice routines are a whole lot more sensible.

don't carry a tension suitcase

The more you practice the better you get. Right? Depends. The problem begins when you try to cram too much into your practice sessions. Incessant practicing invariably leads to a tense mental and physical state that can totally work against you. It gets programmed into your drumming and becomes your *tension baggage*, which gets opened up every time you play. Being nervous before a gig is different. This can be part and parcel of playing and psyches you up to get adrenaline flowing. When you get on stage and let rip, all this energy is then channeled and released naturally.

Learning how to tell these two apart is essential because having pre-show nerves is not the same as carrying around tension baggage.

know when to quit

Your practice sessions should be approached in such a way as to develop and improve all of your abilities at a steady pace, and in a consistently relaxed frame of mind. Never forget the following because it is one of the most important keys to open up your playing: <u>relaxed practice = relaxed performance</u>!

Some students of mine are extremely keen and super ambitious and just as I did in my formative playing years, they set themselves punishing practice schedules. These drummers are of the opinion that if someone else practices two hours a day, then they have to go one better and do three hours a day, no matter what! I've learned and believe the only thing that over-practicing achieves is to cause your playing to become stale, due to a tense and uptight state of mind.

I am the first to encourage <u>ambition</u> and purport it to be a vital ingredient for <u>success</u>. I also advocate <u>consistency</u> to be one of the essential keys for continual growth and improvement. But when this changes to obsession and is not kept in check, then it's time to take a closer look.

For example: You're practicing snare drum technique and have been going at it for a long time, your hands and arms are really tired and you're experiencing pain – YES it's time to STOP! Don't think along the lines of "wow, I'm really working my arms and hands here, this has got to be good for endurance, I'll just push it another twenty minutes". NO NO NO! The fact that there is pain means that you have exhausted your muscles and tested them to the limit. More excessive pounding is not going to achieve anything productive because tension is building and it's time to take that break. If you intend to carry on later that's fine, but not before refreshing yourself and letting the tension subside.

Similarly, if you're practicing reading exercises at 2am and your eyes feel as though they need matchsticks to keep them open, but you insist on carrying on till 2:30am because that was the time you set your allocated practice session to end – then that too is ridiculous. Put down the sticks, close the book and go to sleep! Tomorrow is another day and you can carry on where you left off in a fresher, more alert frame of mind.

If you think that the above examples sound a bit too extreme then let me assure you that they are not. I personally have pushed myself into similar situations and know of other drummers who have fallen prey to these over ambitious practice routines. One such drummer was a friend who at the time, was playing a club residency that used to finish at 2am in the morning. He would then stay in the club for a nightcap or two *socializing*, then arrive home at 3 or 4am, depending on the level of socializing. Instead of getting some rest he would practice, unfortunately not on pads, but sitting on his carpet and banging on the floor working out drum parts for the new songs to be added to the band's Top40 repertoire. My wife (then girlfriend) and I lived two doors away from his apartment so the sound used to travel. Saying she would get slightly irritated by this late night thumping doesn't quite express her feelings and needless to say she'd be at his door expressing herself – colorfully! Not unreasonable since she (and most others in the apartment building) had a day job and needed a good nights rest. Did I mention the dark rings under his eyes? These were truly classic and not very healthy! Had he been sensible and rested he would have been fresher the following day – along with my wife!

to sum up

In defense of over enthusiastic drummers (like myself), it's easy to get carried away and immerse ourselves in something we love. I always encourage consistent practicing and love to see drummers young and old all fired up about their art. Just be aware that this fire can quickly burn out due to excessive over practice.

Most of you are sensible enough to know when to quit, keeping yourself and your playing on an even keel, but I know that there will always be that small contingent of over keen and over ambitious drummers who will burn the candle at both ends.

Like the first sentence of this chapter states:
BE SENSIBLE.

is setting goals relevant to achieving success?

In The Oxford Dictionary the word 'goal' is defined as *an object of effort*. For me this translates into having something worthwhile to aim for, encouraging and giving us a direction to follow in order to successfully realize our dreams.

Ask any 'hungry' musician what his or her ultimate objective in life is, and they'll almost certainly reply that it's to be rich and famous. Great. There's absolutely nothing wrong with this goal, the problem is that most really don't have a clue how they're going to achieve it. They broadly think that if they just practice enough and (somehow) manage to join the right band, this will be all that's needed. Fair enough, for some this has happened and (with a bit of luck) it might just happen to you.

The reality is that most musicians religiously and blindly practice away, drifting in and out of various bands, waiting and hoping for that lucky break to come their way. The elusive break may just jump out of the blue, but I believe a surer bet is to set a route or path of goals to follow, and strive for what you want to accomplish. This applies to bands and individuals alike, since we all have a product to sell. As a musician you set your goal(s) to where you personally want to be as a drummer and as a band collectively agree to make one choice on what you all would like to achieve.

the bedroom musician syndrome

There is that contingent of musicians who sit forever in their bedrooms practicing and practicing, and do nothing about getting out there and playing with other people. They too, as if

THE BEDROOM MUSICIAN

by magic, expect to be rewarded for all their hours of dedicated practice and that the right band will come to them. Let's get one thing straight – you and only you can make things happen for you.

I'm sure every one of us knows or has known a bedroom musician. I knew a rock guitarist who spent hours in his room running his scales, playing to songs, recording his ideas on demos and so on. I'd walk past his house and hear this incredible guitar playing and wonder when he was going to get out there and play. Countless times I'd ask when he planned to do this and his answer was always, "when I feel I'm ready, I'll get round to it". He never did, and the last time I saw him he still hadn't left his bedroom. What a waste!

Beware! Don't fall into this trap and wait for things to come to you. Think about what you want to accomplish, set your goals, and work with all your dedication toward achieving them.

how to plan your route

Without getting too deep and technical about the mechanics of goal setting, I'll give you a brief but adequate outline on how this process works.

When you think about what you want to accomplish (your goals), you use what is known as forebrain thinking. This is the thought process used in your daily activities such as deciding what to wear, what to eat, where to go, talking on the phone etc. In short, all these actions are applied by *conscious* thought effort.

Once you've consciously decided what you want to accomplish, then it's time to hand over the information to your *unconscious* mind. This faculty is that part of your brain that works in the same way as a computer and will accept anything you *program* into it. Programming takes place by feeding your *conscious* thoughts into your *unconscious* mind by one or both of the following methods:

Creative visualization – *seeing* yourself in the position you'd like to be. This means forming a picture in your mind, performing and experiencing what, how and where you'd like to be. For example: if your goal is to play in a successful rock band then see yourself playing in front of a huge audience to the standard of musicianship that you're striving to reach. *Feel* and enjoy the sensation of being on that stage and *live it out*, as though it were happening in real life. Basically all you're doing is closing your eyes and daydreaming, using the power of your imagination to turn these dreams into reality.

Extreme logical thinkers have a problem believing in this concept because they think it smacks of fairy tales. Well consider this: when a car designer comes up with a new model where does he first see it? Before anything can be solidified by transferring it to paper, he must have an <u>idea</u> first, and this comes from one place – a mind thought – his *imagination*.

Affirmation. By repeating your goal over and over to yourself it gets ingrained into your daily thinking. You can repeat the goal aloud or in your thoughts. Aloud is better as it's almost the same as someone else constantly repeating it to you (which is exactly how brainwashing works). Therefore in essence, you are brainwashing yourself into believing that you will achieve your goals.

Solidify your goals

Don't just carry your goals around in your head either, because thoughts change all the time. Make them concrete by committing them to paper. By seeing your goals written down in front of you they take on a more permanent nature and are also open to review at any time. Pin them on your wall and when you wake up in the morning read through your goals and reinforce your positive driving attitude by always knowing where you're headed, and what you have to do in order to get there. I liken this to the procedure good sales representatives use in order to accomplish a day's worth of meetings and appointments. Without planning ahead they wouldn't have a clue where to start and when to finish, in order to successfully realizing their objective.

When I, (after much conscious thought) decided to go ahead with writing this book, I *mapped out* on paper a route to follow and listed all the steps to climb. These steps were the short-term goals I needed to accomplish along the way in order to reach and finally realize my major long-term goal – which, of course, was to have you reading this book. There is no way I could have achieved this without first having a plan, illustrating and making clear where I was headed, how I was going to do it and what my deadlines were.

To make your goals work they have to contain these key elements:

• you have to establish where you're going and what you want to achieve. This is the end objective – your <u>major goal</u>;

- you have to give yourself a due date – your <u>deadline</u>. By telling yourself when you want to arrive at your goal you create a sense of urgency in order to accomplish this. However, be sensible, give yourself a reasonable time frame;
- your goal has to be <u>positive</u> by using phrases such as '*I am*', '*I will*', '*I do*', '*I can*' and so on – leave no room for doubt;
- aside from your long-term major goal you'll need a progressive list of <u>short-term goals</u> to propel you along the route to your final objective;
- your goals have to be <u>realistic</u> and attainable causing you to stretch your abilities and improve all the time. If they are far fetched and out of your reach you will soon give up;
- your goals should be <u>specific</u> and to the point.

putting it all into practice

Example one: You've decided to go on a journey. You haven't decided on a destination but definitely know that you're going somewhere... Anywhere. Now, in order for you to arrive at a destination you have to know where you're going and how long it is going to take you. Otherwise, you'll just keep on going around in circles without knowing where and when to stop. Now let's apply this same logic to music.

You're an absolute beginner and have said to yourself, "my goal is.... um...err...to be a good drummer"! Ok, so let me ask you this – how good is good? Good to you may be mediocre to me and vice versa. Here's another – when will you be good? As a beginner you'll more than likely have a favorite drummer you look up to and who has inspired you to take up drumming. Therefore, use this person as your *goal*. Get more specific and give yourself a time period in which to accomplish this goal. Say something like: "in five years time I *will* play as well as *xxx* (*your favorite drummer*)". This is now your specific <u>long-term</u> goal. You have a <u>destination</u> – which is to play as well as your chosen drummer, so you know <u>where</u> you're headed. You have also created a <u>time period</u> in knowing when you want to arrive at your destination, which is five years. Further, by using the words <u>I will</u> instead of <u>I want</u> you are being positive and have made up your mind that you will be as good in five years time – or maybe sooner – this of course depends on the drumming ability of your chosen drummer and what steps you take along your route to reach their level of skill.

Example two. You're a good rock drummer but have only

played with a little known local band. Your favorite band is a well-known rock outfit, which has had some chart success and your goal is to definitely play with them. Now, while you've set a very specific goal, unless there is even a remote chance of their present drummer ever leaving, then your goal will remain permanently unrealistic and out of your reach – therefore, you can never reach it.

Rather say, "I will play for a band like *xxx* and achieve the same level of success". Now your goal is (still) specific, but realistic and also attainable... if you practice smart and put in the required time and effort. You can now set about looking for the right musicians to form your own band, or think of ways to let people know who you are in order to join the right, similar type of band. And who knows, your favorite band may one day require a new drummer and due to your efforts in one or both of these strategies and the reputation you have built, they may give you a call offering <u>you</u> the job, or at the very least the chance to audition.

The above two examples are hypothetical scenarios so here's a real life example in how specific goal setting worked tremendously. In 2005 one of my beginner female drum students, in only her fourth lesson, expressed a desire to become the drummer of an all-female theater Revue. In giving herself just under two years to achieve this goal, Laura had set herself a very adventurous target. Adventurous yes... but not impossible.

There were two very important elements present in her dream from the start – she had a very clear vision of her destination and had a workable time frame in which to get there. She also had a solid means to work out what short-term goals were required to arrive at her main destination. Additionally, she had also checked out the market (competition) to know what level was required for her to realize her major goal.

The <u>destination</u> (goal) was 'Girl Talk – The Revue'. The <u>deadline</u> was the 2007 season of the show. The <u>short-term</u> goals were clearly set out for her in our lessons, so that she would be mentally and physically prepared to audition when the time arrived. She knew her <u>market</u> because she had seen the show many times and was aware of the demands required of the drummer.

Laura believed beyond doubt that she would reach her major goal. She systematically worked toward this and when the time came for her to audition for the show, she clinched it hands down. In fact, the Revue had already run six seasons and the show's producer commented that she was the most able drummer they had ever auditioned.

In being clear in her goal and putting in the necessary work, Laura realized her dream and enjoyed a fantastic six-month experience. When the show came to an end she became a permanent member of a busy all-female band that plays high profile corporate functions and events. Inspired? You should be!

as you progress your goals may change

Goal setting only works when you have a progressive route of not too easy, but realistic and attainable short-term goals. By successfully accomplishing them one step at a time, you steadily move forward to realize your long-term major goal. You may find as you progress along your chosen route of short-term goals that your original long-term goal changes in outlook. Because of this you may even eliminate some of your short-term goals or add new ones. Is this acceptable? Of course it is, because what you're doing as you progress along your route is modifying and keeping your long-term goal desirable and accessible for yourself. Life changes all the time and outer circumstances can cause you to make appropriate changes to your long and short-term goals. My original long-term goal looked something like this:

"*I am a successful drummer working with various artists on tours and in the studio. I am also involved in the production side of the recording process*".

This goal, as you can see, what pretty 'session' orientated. I found that the more involved I got in this area, the less I began to enjoy this side of the music business. Now, don't get me wrong – I love recording and the challenge of the studio environment, but more so when part of a team (band) or working on my own projects. I'm happier when I have more creative input and control as to what goes down on tape and also when I have a say on the end result – the final mix. In most cases the final word and decisions regarding any aspect of the session always rests with whoever has hired me. I appreciate this because, after all, they're the people paying for the studio time and also my session fee. I get hired because the artist or producer has faith in my ability to get the job done satisfactorily, so I play what <u>they</u> want to hear. Other people thrive in this type of situation so there is no right or wrong way; it is purely down to the individual drummer's personality.

So, aside from the session fee, I realized that this area of my goal was not as attractive as I had first thought. It became an obsolete part of my long-term goal, which I duly modified. This doesn't mean that I now refuse to do any sessions; rather it's a case of doing projects where I know I'll be included more in the creative process.

the burned out club

Don't listen to people who try to discourage you from achieving your goals. They may tell you that whatever you're trying to achieve is too difficult and way out of your reach and that it won't happen for you – just as it never happened for them.

I've met a lot of musicians in my career and the ones who are the least encouraging are those who belong to what I call the 'burned out' club. They're the ones who never achieved what they wanted, usually due to their own inept attitudes and bad choices. As a result, they continually go round in circles and land up very bitter and unsuccessful. They don't want to see anyone else succeeding where they failed to accomplish and so do their utmost to discourage you. Watch out for members of the burned out club – they're everywhere and usually pretty easy to recognize as they scoff at everything and are continually miserable.

changing attitude

Just before this chapter closes, I'd like to give another example of a bedroom musician – but with a rather different end to the story.

I knew a jazz guitarist who for years sat around in his London flat complaining about the injustices of the music business – how he just couldn't seem to find the right band and how unfair everything was for him. At the time he also had taken out a subscription to the burned out club, because he could be very discouraging to other musicians. The basic truth was that he never opened up the opportunities available to him. He sat at home practicing and expected something good to come to him – "and why not"? he said, "I'm good enough". Well no doubt about that – his playing was excellent, but his attitude wasn't.

We lost contact and I didn't see him for a long time. When I met up with him again I had the pleasure of meeting a changed man. He wasn't just in one band – but three! The first being his money earner working in a posh night club playing jazz and funk cover tunes; the second was a radical three piece power rock outfit comprising two *name* musicians; the third was an avant garde jazz outfit which was totally his own vehicle. In this band he wrote all the material, booked the venues, organized the musicians, arranged publicity, etc. Now how about that for a turnaround and shift in attitude? All because he realized that it was up to him to get off his butt and make things happen, and as you can see... they sure did. If that wasn't enough, he was also writing a musical score for a local amateur theater production! The last time I spoke to him he told me that he was jetting off on a holiday – need I say more?

to sum up

By setting goals, you consciously and unconsciously set your creative wheels in motion, propelling yourself forward in seeking out and opening up opportunities. Waiting for someone else to make things happen is usually a waste of time because your interests are always best served by you.

Virtually all personal achievement, is down to your own efforts.

Try the goal setting ideas presented in this chapter and run with them – they do work.

using other drummers as role models

We all have our favorite drummers and it's from these players that we receive our inspiration. These role models play an important part in shaping the way we play and how we develop our musical personalities.

Virgil Donati's amazing 'power drumming' techniques inspire me to head for the practice room and improve my chops and then Steve Smith fires me up with his subtle approach and style of performance. They are both incredible drummers but with totally different approaches and techniques. Likewise, Vinnie Colaiuta is a genius but then so is Terry Bozzio – two very unlike players and you can't say who's the better of the two because they both possess phenomenal skills.

All great drummers play their own way because they each took a certain personal route or path to achieve their goals and level of playing – and each one in turn had their own personal role models who inspired them to success.

one influence or more?

I'm the type of drummer who has had role models in many different music styles, but this applies to me personally. Alternatively, I've known other drummers who have modeled themselves on just one drummer, in one particular style of music. One such drummer I knew loved the late great John Bonham's drumming. This drummer's name was Mike and he also had the nickname 'Bonzo', which as you may or may not know, was the nickname that John Bonham had. *Bonzo* Mike was in a

rock band doing a lot of Led Zeppelin material and played and tuned his drums as close to John Bonham's signature sound as he could. I suppose Mike was in a sense really just cloning John Bonham. But that's okay because it's what he wanted to do and another thing that was certain was whenever someone mentioned the name Bonzo in the music circle I moved in, we all knew who was being discussed – Bonzo Mike had created his *own* identity.

a personal example

In my formative playing years being the Carl Palmer fanatic that I was, I took it upon myself to work out and play to all Emerson Lake and Palmer (ELP) recorded material. As a result I painstakingly spent hour upon hour deciphering Carl's amazing solo on Tank off the first album. I memorized the whole of *Tarkus – Trilogy* that presented some odd time challenges; I blew my brains out on *Brain Salad Surgery*; drummed along to Carl's musically diverse solo side 3 on *Works Vol.1* etc etc. In short I digested it all. As a result of all this effort, one night I received the biggest compliment I could have hoped for at that time.

I was leaving the stage after having played a set that featured a drum solo when a member of the audience walked up to me and said just two words, 'Carl Palmer'. Hey now, those two words to me really struck home because once we got talking I discovered that he was an avid ELP buff and really knew his stuff. My solo had not been a carbon copy of Carl's playing but rather contained some of his trade-marks which I played with my own interpretation; and the fact that this person had recognized this made it all the more self satisfying.

As small or even trivial as this compliment may seem to some, for me this was a huge step forward and the basis for further continual improvement and recognition. I knew then that I had reached a major goal in establishing a new and higher standard of playing for myself.

to sum up

So, which is right – one role model or many? I think that's up to the individual. I moved from one specific role model to the next, until eventually, I ended up with many influences from many diverse styles of music. Now I listen to anyone and everyone

using other drummers as role models

I like the sound of. Is this musical maturity? Who knows? But one thing I know for sure is that having specific role models will shape your playing, as their drumming style and ability level will help you to measure the progress in your own performance.

how to keep on being enthusiastic

The routine of practicing exercises over and over again can sometimes cause us to lose interest in the drums, resulting in us becoming bored and diminishing our desire to sit down and play. So how do we keep up this desire for drumming and sustain enthusiasm for practice. How do we turn the necessity of repetition into an interesting and stimulating routine?

the boredom factor

One day Fred, the guitar player in my very first band was watching me play an exercise over and over. After a while he posed this question: "Don't you ever get bored with that?" he asked, "you're just playing the same thing over and over." To be honest, at the time I couldn't think of a good answer and simply came out with an emphatic "NO". It never occurred to me that what I was doing could ever be boring. I loved the drums, and practicing to me was just another part of something I loved.

Was this merely the innocence of youth tempered by pure unadulterated optimism... mmm I wonder? I think part of it had something to do with that, however I've come to realize that my biggest motivator was the intense desire I possessed (and still do) to continually improve and be the best. As I got better and better, this progress fuelled my desire for the drums and fired my enthusiasm to practice more and more. All the countless repetitions involved in my daily practice routine were just part and parcel of playing the drums – after all, you can't get bored with something you love can you? Actually... you can. But, coupled with the advice given in Chapter Four on sensible practice techniques and the following suggestions, you can reduce this risk.

Creativity defeats boredom

Lets check out an example to illustrate this:

You're sitting there... doing countless repetitions of rudiments, when you find yourself becoming bored. You think to yourself, "man, this sucks, it's true what they say about rudiments, they're boring and I'm just playing the same thing over and over". Okay, fair enough, this might be true, but let's look at a fresh take on this attitude:

Think about what's happening – if whatever you're practicing really sounds good to you and you're satisfied that it sounds right, then perhaps you've spent enough time on this? But... then again... can you play it at different tempos, starting at the slowest possible speed to the quickest time where it still sounds and feels good? What about dynamics – can you play it very quietly right through to a very loud volume level? If there are accented notes, are they being articulated correctly in relation to the unaccented notes? All good so far? Cool! If you can play this rudiment you're practicing incredibly well on snare drum, then can you apply it to the whole drum set? No? Then start getting creative and think how you can split this pattern up between the different components on your set-up, and also between your four limbs. Now the combinations will start to flow and that boring singular rudiment takes on a whole different challenge. Incidentally: In my teachings I will start to explore the possibilities of applying rudiments to the drum set, only once a student can effectively play this proficiently on one surface – like snare drum or a practice pad. The object of this kind of investigative exercise would be to explore how many ways you can make these expanded patterns become part of your playing library or arsenal.

As you see... the possibilities are virtually endless and you only become bored if *you* let yourself become bored. A further example of this is a fact that I can keep a (serious) student busy on only the first page of George L Stone's 'Stick Control' book for a year, by exploring the many ways that those simple one line exercises can be applied to 4 way independence between all four limbs.

I still, after over 30 years of playing, sit down to practice.

But as my time now is extremely limited, I ensure that I only work on relevant study material to improve weak areas. For example, if I feel that my playing is slipping and sounding sloppy, I purposely practice and tighten this up by using relevant material and exercises. My other practice is implemented into my everyday involvement with music whether it be performing, teaching, visualizing, listening, or whatever else I find myself doing in this area.

The will to continually improve defeats boredom

Being an avid reader of drumming magazines and reading interviews with famous name drummers, I am constantly amazed at the comments and reservations they make about their playing. Some who have excellent timing will say that they are still striving to improve in this area, while others with amazing feel say that this can be bettered.

The truth is that the best drummers in the world are never entirely satisfied with their playing, as they feel that there is always something that can be improved or bettered. Nobody's perfect and anyway, if you think you know it all and have nothing left to learn, where's the motivation going to come from?

What about you?

So where does your motivation come from? What fuels your desire for the drums?

We all have different motivating factors. Quite simply, I call them motivators. As mentioned before, I believe all drummers start out wanting to emulate their favorite drummer or drummers. Then some carry on doing it for the money alone, others for the stardom, some for the perks of the job (such as groupies) and others will do it purely for the love of playing music. Most musicians play music due to a combination of all these reasons/motivators – but to reach your pinnacle of success, how would you continually bounce back when faced with setback after setback?

Motivator #1 – Fortune. I'll start by saying that if your only motivating factor for playing music is to make a lot of money then you've made a pretty terrible career choice. Rather look at becoming a lawyer or engineer as these are much more secure routes to making good bucks. Drummers out there who earn their living from playing music, especially the 'free-lancers', will agree that the unemployment factor can at times be somewhat high. Sure, it's great when you're in work and earning, but the other side of the coin where you suddenly find yourself without a job always looms large and is an unpleasant reality.

I personally have experienced the frustration and shock of being on what I thought was a *safe and secure* tour, only to receive an early morning call to hear that the whole thing has been canceled due to poor ticket sales, or whatever reason – contract or no contract. And I would have canceled other work to do this *safe* tour!

Musicians who regularly do residency type work such as lounge bars in hotels or cabaret clubs, will agree that whenever there is a problem regarding low attendance, the first factor to be blamed is the band. Invariably it's always the band's fault, because they aren't playing the right material, or they're slacking off, or the sound isn't right or... whatever excuse the management can *drum up* (sorry, couldn't resist the pun!). So if your only motivator is money then I urge you to have a rethink.

Laying your hands on the big moola is of course possible, but as you should now be aware, only a small number of musicians ever hit the jackpot. So in light of this consider how you would react if, due to whatever reason or reasons you don't make the grade – what then? Will this be a big enough blow to cause you to give up playing, or would the life of a working pro drummer suffice, where a decent living can be earned without necessarily being a mega-star? In other words, could you hit the road with a good, well paid covers band and play the length and breadth of your state or county? Or how about a sophisticated nightclub gig; or seeing the world for free by backing cabaret artists on a cruise ship? A good living can be earned if you're smart, take good care of business and are able to cut it musically.

I once played a six-month Holiday Inn residency, which was a stones throw away from a hot sandy beach. We had free accommodation with each member of the band having their own room with TV and video. The deal also included three free meals a day and a good salary. Our repertoire consisted of original songs and also cover tunes of our choice. We were a good rock band and I had a great time! Would a gig like this do it for you?

Motivator #2 – *Aiming for the top*. I often get asked by younger drummers and also mature beginners, who I think the best drummer in the world is. I have to apologize because I don't have an answer. I do however have my favorites. Some are *better* or even considered the *best* in one genre, while others the *best* in many different genres, but as for the best drummer in the world? Mmmm, you tell me.

Wanting to be the best at what you do is a great motivating factor. The music business is highly competitive and only the best and most devoted survive its challenges. To survive, you have to give your utmost 100% effort to compete at the highest level. For me personally, wanting to be best translates into being the best musician that I can possibly be at any given time. This attitude (and goal) can never exhaust itself because there will always be something new to learn and master.

Motivator #3 – Fame. My concept of fame once again boils down to relativity. For example: You may be a really well known drummer in the city, county, state, or even country you live in and enjoy the same level of recognition as an internationally famous drummer – albeit on a smaller scale! I've met many musicians who are quite content to be *famous* in their own territory, however large or small.

One of my major goals many years ago was to be recognized and respected by my peers, more so than achieving public recognition. I know that I've accomplished my first (industry recognition) objective, but I have also achieved a very respectable public recognition as I have been fortunate to appear on TV many times, frequently appeared in various music press and have also conducted radio and TV interviews.

A further example of how relative fame can be was when I was playing in a UK country band that had won the BCMA 'Best Band' award four times. Even though I was in a band that was being televised on CMTV Europe as far a field as Russia, headlining major festivals and appearing month after month in relevant music press, if you had asked an 18 year old metal drummer who I was, they would have looked at you with a puzzled look on their face and replied "who"? This is purely because he or she wouldn't have been *plugged* into the scene that I was in at that time.

Every area or genre of music has its sole listenership or audience and often will not cross over into other styles – and this applies to even the big names. Ask out and out *rockers* whether they've heard of Aaron Neville or Gino Vannelli and you'll probably just get another "who?".

So the question is, am I satisfied with my achievements? Well yes, I am proud of what I've accomplished, but musically I

still have many things I want to do. At the time of this rewrite of *Rhythm of the Head*, I'm venturing into solo album territory, getting involved in library music for radio and TV, expanding on the drum clinic side of things for myself, and more...

As you can see, I am not resting on any laurels (whatever others perceive them to be). I'm excited about the new things I am getting into and looking toward new horizons. So I have new major goals to fuel my desire and enthusiasm. And by the time you read this book, who knows what inroads I will have made into these areas?

two more motivators!

Aside from the three main motivators; Fame, Fortune and Aiming for the Top – there are two additional motivators of a more general nature.

Motivator (A) – Mixing with the best. I find that I perform at my best when surrounded by the best musicians available. They keep me on my toes through my desire of wanting to rise and match their high standard of musicianship, also ensuring that I don't become bored. Complacency can sometimes set in when playing with musicians who pull you down creatively. This can result in you becoming dissatisfied with your playing and/or working situation.

Motivator (B) – Other drummers. Drummers are generally more likely to socialize and mix with each other than musicians who play other instruments. I'm not quite sure why this is, but there seems to be a bond that draws drummers together to support and befriend each other. I think this is so cool! Maybe it's due to us so very often being treated as *non-musicians* and normally being stuck at the back on stage. What I do believe is that it takes a different sort of individual to play drums. How many other professions can you think of (aside from boxing!), where you get paid for beating the hell out of something? Ha!

Mixing with other drummers motivates us through our exchange of ideas and sense of comradeship. Also, seeing and hearing other drummers playing up a storm at gigs and clinics is another great motivating factor. I love drum clinics –not only in being able to learn and be inspired by the clinician, but equally due to the presence of the other drummers in the room, which creates a positive energy in causing us to want to sit down and practice.

avoid extremes

Whatever your objectives, just be careful not to take anything to extremes. For example: if your chief (and only) motivator is money, you may become so engrossed with the material side that you neglect to take care of the music side. Your playing standard could deteriorate so badly that as an unwelcome result, you find yourself being fired due to your incompetence! Alternatively, should you fail to take care of business and find yourself laden down with unpaid bills, eviction notices and an empty fridge, then you've tipped the scales to the other extreme. This scenario happened to me in 1984 at Christmas in London. My most vivid and painful recollection of that period was driving to a pawn shop with a pile of records from my beloved vinyl collection and having to pawn them for £20 (around $38). If I hadn't managed to pawn them I wouldn't have had enough money to put in a bit of gas to get home! My wife's Christmas present that year was a bar of chocolate! I swore after that experience that I would take much better care of business!!

to sum up

Remember, boredom and complacency can be kept at bay. Consider the Motivators in this chapter, apply them to your personal situation and ensure that you're constantly fired up to perform at your utmost best.

money or art?

I believe that musicians whether professional or amateur, can be categorized into two main groups. One being money orientated and the other art orientated. Do you know which one you are? More than likely you're a combination of the two, but the question is on which side do you place more emphasis.

the art side

Sounds dumb I know, but if you're the type of drummer who is happy to venture out for little or sometimes no money out of *preference*, then you lean toward the 'arty' side. To clarify: As long as you can eat, pay your rent and bills, but most importantly play the music you love – then you're happy being an 'artist'.

I'll give an example here by sticking my neck out with reference to jazz musicians... I believe the majority of jazz drummers will agree when I say that this genre of music generally doesn't pay that well. Jazz musicians play jazz because that's what they love to play – and don't compromise, however small the pay packet. So it's no strange phenomenon to find that jazz musicians will probably play music as a hobby or sideline to their day jobs. So is that it you may ask, are all jazz players doomed to a penniless existence? Of course not.

There are elite *jazzers* such as Chick Corea, Billy Cobham and Pat Metheny who have built successful and respected reputations on the *art* side, but also managed to make it financially viable. So how have they done this? Well, they may have involved

themselves in other work, related to what they love to do, but which pays much more. Steve Gadd (if you don't know who he is you ain't a drummer) is an example of a hugely successful drummer who has recorded and toured with the biggest names in the world. This involvement afforded him to record and head up his own jazz and funk orientated bands – 'Stuff' and 'Gadds Gang'. Additionally, he has won industry polls and awards and endorses top of the range musical gear. Therefore to me, it spells out that he and other similarly successful jazz orientated musicians are members of that elite 5%.

But compare the rewards to be earned by a drummer who has *made it* to the elite 5% in the rock or pop field and the difference can be quite staggering. This is because the budgets of major jazz business deals pale in comparison to major rock tours and record deals. The reason for this is quite simple. Compared to rock or country, jazz has a minority listening audience and it is the number of CD and ticket sales that dictate everything financial in the music business. So no matter how phenomenal your playing, if you choose a minority music genre, what you can expect in return is a minority audience and a smaller paycheck. Common sense?

crossing over

Purists are those musicians who don't entertain the idea of playing (or even listening to) anything else but their chosen genre. Cool, I haven't got a problem with this because I tend to be pretty choosy in what I like to play and also listen to. The problem starts when purists insist on telling other musicians what to do. You see many jazz purists will say that taking on other work outside of jazz is *selling out*. I don't agree. The motivating factor or factors causing any drummer to seek out greater financial return from their work is valid and personal to the individual concerned. I would never tell you what your motivators should be and I trust you would do the same for me. Doing what you need to do in order to survive in this business, is your own business.

Incidentally, you don't find purists only in jazz. No way, you'll find country purists, Latin purists, classical purists and then the *extreme* purist who will only involve himself in one area of jazz, or country, or whatever. This is another whole books worth of discussion, so I'll make a sensibly quiet exit out of this area right here.

the money side

I've known many musicians and singers who signed that elusive record company deal and still struggled to make ends meet – I was one of them! This is because you only start making real money once the advance from the record company has been paid back in full. Sadly, many signed bands never survive to reach this solvent point. In situations like this where an adequate income was not produced, I found other (music industry) related means of making a living. On the other hand you only need to go to Los Angeles and discover that every barman or waitress you meet is an actor. Each to their own!

As this chapter focuses on how to make the music business work financially, I am now going to discuss the pros and cons of playing cover music as opposed to original music. Most *working* musicians earn their living playing somebody else's music. This can range from a drummer playing in a Top 40 covers club band to a session musician who freelances for various *original* artists. Both are required to play someone else's music, the big difference is that the session player will more than likely be getting a bigger pay packet as he or she is working for the original artist. However, this is not always the case. I've known some cover band musicians who have also made a lot of money. Of course this is all dependent on what level work they've managed to secure.

Top 40 club cover musicians and lounge acts often get a lot of flak from original music musicians. They claim that cover band musicians aren't *true* musicians. This depends how you look at it. True, these covers musicians may not be as creative in the sense of writing original material, but a lot of the time these covers musicians will be better players, as they will have involved themselves in a myriad of musical activities to keep on working – perhaps even playing original music at some point. Many cover band musicians are ex original band musicians who have decided to take this route because they may have gotten married and need more security, or have exhausted all possibility of making it as an original musician, or are still gunning to try get their music signed but are working in a Holiday Inn lounge to earn a living. There is no definitive route. If there were an ideal way to get signed and make great money while attempting to do this then everybody would be doing it.

It's not wrong to play cover band music and right to play

original music, or vice versa – it's what your specific situation requires you to do in order to survive. There are many successful signed original bands that were cover bands before they got signed – Van Halen being one of them! They were a happening rock covers band before exploding onto the international rock scene with their own music. And then you find successful original bands where from the start, they wrote and played only their music – U2 is one of these bands. But not even legendary bands like the Beatles and the Rolling Stones played only original music when they started out – they mixed covers with their own music, which by the way, is the route that most bands take to build a loyal following and fan base. One of the most successful bands I played with and which recorded three albums, mixed covers and original music when starting out.

So as you see, money orientated musicians playing other peoples music for a living can also be original art orientated musicians, and the two can co-exist quite happily. In fact some may consider this kind of musician to be even more art orientated as their entire lifestyle is music based, rather than the original musician who holds down a non music related job in the day because he refuses to play anybody else's music but his own. Hey, both attitudes are correct as this depends on the individual concerned and their surrounding circumstances!

I personally could never hack splitting my life into two separate entities, in being the musician and the 'nine to fiver'. Even working in a music store was hard for me to accept. I basically wanted to only play music, which is what I did for many years – live and in the studio. This kept alive my motivation in always being involved in music no matter what I was playing, whether original or covers material. However, after many years of doing this I decided to come off the road and settle down a bit. Now my main *gig* is education (teaching), which I mix with playing, writing and recording. What a great lifestyle!

to sum up

A performer may start out more money orientated and find that with time and experience, shifts towards the art orientated side – or visa versa. No way is right or wrong, as your career motivators are yours and yours alone to choose.

how to deal effectively with criticism

You walk off stage having played what you think is a great set, when someone walks up to you and says, "hey, what's up, I didn't think you played well tonight".

How do you react? Do you just shrug it off or do you allow this comment to stick in your mind and bug you?

outside criticism

Criticism from an outside source can be very disheartening and even destructive if you take it to heart and let it eat away at your self-confidence. The thing to remember is that these comments will only affect you to the degree in which you believe them to be true. What this means is that if the comment has come from someone who you know to be knowledgeable (in other words a good drummer you respect and look up to or someone you know), then listen closely to their comments and learn. They are trying to help and as long as you don't let what they say rip you apart then there is no problem.

Now a comment or criticism coming from a totally uninformed source is a different situation – remember 'Professors of music' in Chapter Two. In a situation like this where someone is trying to tell you how to play without having the first clue what to do themselves, then as politely as you can manage, brush them off. These people are often closet musicians in that they'd love to be able to do what you're doing and in overcoming their jealousy or guilt complex, insist on ripping you apart – ignore them!

self criticism

Now, totally different and a lot more dangerous, is your own criticism. Watch out for this one because if you entertain it, this can be extremely destructive and tear your self-confidence apart. Statements like *'I don't play well'*; *'I can't do this'*; *'I hate my drumming'*; *'I'll never be good enough'*; *'I'll never get this right'*, etc. Self criticism is one of the biggest factors, if not the biggest factor in holding us back and preventing us from playing to our full potential. I view this brand of criticism as self punishment, because what you do when you continually attack yourself with negative statements is ensure that your performance will be anything but good. So instead of punishing yourself you should ask "why"? – "Why do I do this? – Why did I make that mistake? – Why don't I play this well"? Could it be because you lacked focus or concentration, or maybe you set yourself up to make a mistake by worrying beforehand about making the mistake? Perhaps you were just so frozen by tension that it inhibited free flow of mental and physical control?

getting to the root cause or causes

It's healthy practice to be able to identify and accept your shortcomings and to then maturely set out and act upon a course of action to rectify these mistakes. For example: If you've identified your mistake or mistakes due to miscounting, then perhaps you could work through one, or all of these three suggestions.

1. If you're continually making mistakes when working through reading material, then slow down the tempo and try playing the exercise first to only a quarter note count which will of course be 1 2 3 4. Then move onto an eighth note count being 1 an 2 an 3 an 4 an. Finally, play to a sixteenth note 1e+ah (e-and-ah) 2e+ah 3e+ah 4e+ah count. In doing this (depending on the material you're reading), your awareness of all the notes (and rests) is heightened as your focus changes with each different counting system. Then if you're really keen and want to make this even more challenging, you can try counting only the rests between the played notes. This really opens up your awareness of not only the notes that should be physically played, but the (un-played) space between these notes. As the famous classical composer Claude Debussy wisely quoted: "music is the space between the notes".

2. If you miscounted due to losing your way while playing

a song, then try this exercise: Without physically playing, listen to the song and write out the number of measures (bars) in each section. Pay close attention to the song's form as to where the verses, choruses, middle eight, etc start and end. Focus also on any changes in feel and groove, and the nature of the fills when moving from one section to another. How many verses are there? How long is the intro and does it repeat anywhere in the song? Is the last chorus single or double?

By engaging in this form of *listening* practice, you expand your musical ear and reduce the risk of losing your place in a song because you can identify each section from a musical standpoint.

3. To improve your general time on the drum set switch on your metronome and play through various feels, beats and fills that you regularly use in your playing. As you play, make a point of counting through your fills, ensuring you give each one its full length to reduce the risk of coming out before or after where you should come back into the groove. Start with simple grooves and fills and increase the level of difficulty as you become more relaxed and comfortable with this exercise.

In practicing one or all three of the above exercises, you will be zoning in and attacking the root cause or causes of miscounting errors. You're turning weaknesses into strengths and ensuring that these types of mistake will be kept to a minimum. In truth, you can't really predict that mistakes will <u>never</u> happen, because you're only human and all human beings make mistakes. Even finely tuned machines break down from time to time.

negative predictions

Repeating statements such as '*I know I won't do well*', often turns them into self fulfilling prophecies. What you are doing is convincing and setting yourself up to make mistakes. I know that the following is easier said than done, but the antidote to this is to repeat something like '*I will do well*' and picture yourself doing just that. When you can faultlessly play whatever it is you're trying to accomplish in your mind, then transferring it to your limbs is so much easier. For example: If you have an audition coming up and are really struggling to physically play something, then close your eyes and try to picture yourself performing the relevant pattern or song <u>exactly</u> as you want to hear it – without mistakes. If you need to slow this down drastically, then do it. If you still can't *hear* or *see* in your mind what you are trying to play, then this means that you haven't yet internalized what you are attempting to play – in other words it isn't clear in your mind. So if you have a recording of the track then you need to go back and listen more closely to what you are trying to play. If this still doesn't work, then obviously what you're trying to achieve is beyond your present capabilities and you need to seek out the help of a more experienced drummer or teacher.

When you can *hear* and *see* in your mind that which you need to physically play, then allow yourself to *play* this and enjoy a faultless *performance*. After you've successfully completed your performance, then see yourself being told that you've got the job. Does all this sound a bit 'out there'? Don't concern yourself, you'll be checking this out in greater detail in Chapter Twenty Four which deals with Creative Visualization.

the other extreme side of predictions

Just as you want to combat against negative predictions, be careful not to be overly confident or optimistic. Never say "*I will play this perfectly*". By using that word "perfectly", you may well be setting yourself up for even more self punishment. Because if you do play exceptionally well, though make just one mistake, then you won't have played *perfectly*... and as a result, might not be satisfied with your *imperfect* performance. This is not a sensible attitude to entertain.

From the world's greatest performers to the world's worst, we all make mistakes. Hey, it's a basic fact of life – and performance. Accept it. That's why I love to watch shows that feature out-takes of actors, singers, news readers and so on, making a hash of things. This comforts and reminds me just how human we all are.

I remember talking to drummer Mickey Currie who has played with 'Hall and Oates' and also 'Bryan Adams'. He said quite funnily, that whenever he walks into a session or different kind of situation, he wonders if this is the time that he's gonna get "found out" in where he can't do what he's supposed to do. We had a good laugh about that. Of course, every time he did walk into that kind of situation he played great and everything went smoothly. So take comfort from a drummer who has toured the world many times, played stadiums and arenas, recorded drums on some of the biggest hits of all time and played with some of the most famous stars on this planet.

Keep your mind on the ball

In football a player is told to always keep his eye on the ball in order to reduce the risk of mis-kicking – in other words, making a mistake – the same principle applies in performance. If your attention and concentration slips and wanders from what you are doing, the more chance you have of making a mistake.

One major reason why many drummers lose concentration, is that they become overly concerned with what other drummers in the audience may be thinking about their performance. This used to affect me pretty badly in my earlier days when I was often pretty insecure about my drumming and felt I had *something to prove*. So whenever I knew there were other drummers in the audience I'd try to impress them by being flashy – which almost always backfired because I was no longer focusing on playing the music. The pressure I put on myself to come up with that *extra special* drum fill or beat usually caused me to play something way out of the musicality of the song, or something I wasn't too familiar with, resulting in mistakes.

To sum up

By being totally in the now and filling your mind with only one task, which is whatever you are playing at the time, the chance of making mistakes is kept to an absolute minimum. Also, when doing this you prevent any negatives from entering your mind. This keeps you positively charged and should someone question or doubt your playing, you're in a far better frame of mind to effectively deal with this criticism and more importantly, your own self criticism.

positive attitude – do you have it?

The underlying reason why anyone has a negative attitude toward playing the drums is that before they even start playing, they are expecting to make mistakes. And if they do happen to make one or more mistakes, they then tend to dwell too much on those regardless of whether they actually played the rest of the song really well.

So right from the start, the correct attitude to have is to expect to play well and not remotely entertain the idea of making mistakes. And if you do happen to make any, but play the rest of the song fantastically well, then the foremost thought in your mind should be that <u>you played well</u> – with one or two mistakes. In other words, don't fill your mind with the mistakes and forget how good the rest of your playing was! Common sense? Of course it is, but it's amazing how so many forget this – it's easily done and should be avoided at all costs.

Of course you don't ignore the mistakes and pretend they never happened. No, you acknowledge that they were present in your playing, and then set out to put them right – ensuring that the same does not happen again. This subtle difference in attitude is what defines you as either a negative or positive thinker and measures the amount of self confidence you have in your playing, which in turn, defines your performance result.

acknowledgement is the key

Here's a personal example which goes back a good few years to when I was a percussionist in a military band. The

percussion section (which comprised four of us) was given a piece of music to learn and later perform on xylophone in a massed bands display in our local City Hall. The piece, 'On the Track is a very quick solo percussion set piece featuring fast sixteenth note passages throughout and therefore, demands extreme concentration. We were given a month in which to learn and master this piece of music.

After much practice, the day finally arrived for us to play it with the full orchestra in rehearsal. All of us were very nervous to say the least and viewed the next few minutes uneasily. The first drummer shuffled uneasily over to the expectant xylophone. He waited for the count... 1 2 3 4... and away he went. He started well and everything sounded cool, until halfway through, he lost his place. He stopped playing for about eight bars and with a totally confused and anguished expression looked as though he was about to give up. Incidentally, let me assure you that 'On the Track' is not a piece of music to lose your place in, because its quick tempo makes it very difficult to find your way back. The ordeal was soon over and as was customary for solo performances of this kind in rehearsal, the orchestra applauded his performance. He put down the mallets, turned around and walked back towards us, shaking his head with a look of resignation on his face.

Next it was my turn. Dutifully, I squared up to the foreboding instrument constructed of wood and metal. I'd be lying if I said that I felt 100% comfortable with the piece I was about to play, since prior to enlisting in the ILHR (Imperial Light Horse Regiment) Band my tuned percussion experience was extremely limited. In spite of this shortcoming something happened to my attitude just before starting the piece. My nervousness seemed to evaporate as I thought to myself, "well this is it, I'm just going to go for it now, no matter what". The conductor looked at me, tapped his baton and bang, launched us into the piece at what to this day I'm still convinced was a quicker tempo than the previous percussionist had been forced to endure. For the next three minutes I completely blocked out everything but the music I was playing. At the time I was aware of hitting a number of wrong notes, but somehow they seemed unimportant, overshadowed by my go-and-get-'em attitude. I never once paused or faltered, regardless of those bum notes and just played to the best of my ability. At the end of the piece the other orchestra musicians applauded and I returned to my three smiling percussion colleagues.

After the rehearsal we all made our way to the Band bar for a drink, but more importantly to discuss the evening's proceedings. Our commanding officer who earlier had been conducting the band, was full of praise and even bought me a drink – something he had never done before! My percussion section buddies complimented me on how well I'd performed with one of them saying how impressed he was by the positive way I had attacked the piece.

Now out of us four percussionists, I was the least qualified. I joined the unit primarily as a drum set player and also with only three months service under my belt. My colleagues were a whole lot more experienced in this area of percussion. Gary, the leader of our section had been in the Band for over four years and was a good reader and very competent in most areas of percussion. Lindsay was a far better reader than I was and also had previous orchestral experience. And lastly, Bernard was a classically trained percussionist. So if you weigh up the odds, I should have been the one to put out the weakest performance. Instead, I put up a really strong showing that was on par with my more experienced colleagues – or even better.

I truly believe that aside from the practice I'd put in, this result was largely due to my attitude of not worrying about doing badly and not letting the mistakes get in the way of my performance. And the mistakes that did occur were down to my inexperience in xylophone expertise. I acknowledged that the way to cut down on these was to spend more time practicing the instrument – which I did. The result of this was that when we came to eventually play the piece at the show, I played even better.

I'd now like to tell you about a drum clinic I attended quite a few years ago featuring a famous British drummer renowned for his spectacular drum solos...

even the big names falter

I arrived in good time at the venue and entered a room filled with drummers, young and old. When the time arrived for the show to begin, we were informed that this featured drummer had been held up and that the clinic would run late. After a short time he arrived and on stepping out onto the stage, received a huge welcoming round of applause. He acknowledged this warm reception with a smile and then without a word, sat down behind

positive attitude - do you have it?

a glorious double bass drum setup. He started playing his introductory solo but something was wrong. He just didn't look comfortable, or at ease and was coming across as very unsettled. Perhaps the reason causing him to arrive late had something to do with this? The solo, which lasted around eight minutes, was pretty mediocre compared to this great drummer's usual high standard of playing. But nonetheless, the audience of drummers applauded appreciatively and also I felt, out of sense of warm encouragement for their hero – somehow knowing that he was capable of more.

The clinic proceeded with examples shown on different areas of technique, the usual demonstrations on the featured drum gear and also the obligatory question and answer period involving the audience. But while this was all happening I was sensing a change of attitude taking place in this drummer – more positive and more together all the time. Eventually the time came for the clinic to close, but not before the second and last drum solo was played ... and man, what a solo it was! The difference in playing to the first solo was unbelievable. When the last crash was heard ending his performance, the eruption from the audience was a deafening roar, showing their overwhelming appreciation for this master drummer.

The autograph signing session ensured and I managed to have a few words with the man. I put forward the question on the difference between the two solos he had played and how he had felt about them. His answer was that he knew he had started on an unsteady footing, but by possessing an underlying, aggressive positive attitude and also believing that what any audience always remembers is a strong finish, he eliminated the shaky start from his mind. He focused on the rest of the clinic by *pulling out all stops* and doing well, because after all, it was his reputation on the line. The end result was that this attitude won through and I'm convinced that had he let the weak opening dominate his thoughts and get the better of him, then the rest of the clinic would have simply been as mediocre all the way through.

All drummers have their own personalized way of dealing with and sorting out tricky situations. But one constant for all is that mistakes will only be as big and serious as you think they are. The more emphasis you place on them, the more they will cloud your drumming. Also of extreme importance is to remember to direct any aggression you're feeling due to mistakes (negativity) at the actual negativity. Don't hate yourself for making mistakes – hate the mistakes and let your positive thoughts crush them.

By spending enough time and effort filling your head with the correct thoughts, you will cut down on making mistakes. But remember that you are only human and that mistakes will occur, no matter what. So the secret here is in how you deal and ride with them, as this will determine your performance output and level. Again, in other words – it is how you *cover them up*.

You see I've made mistakes on stage where not one member of the audience knew that I had made the mistake, because I covered them up so well. And sometimes not even the other band members realized that I had made any mistake. Granted, this is a learned skill and takes a lot of practice and time spent on stage to achieve. You can also view this as another performance tool, just like any other technique you employ to perform at your utmost best.

I don't expect younger drummers to make head or tail of what I'm outlining here. This is because children, on the whole, don't really know what a negative attitude is. They just openly bash away with little inhibition, not caring what people think. But as we get older, music (and life) takes on a more serious nature and negative experiences can take hold and inhibit us and in some cases ruin promising careers.

think yourself 'GOOD'

There have been times when I have felt a *wave* of negativity threatening to disrupt my playing. When this happens one technique I use to combat this is to think or (depending on the performance situation) verbally repeat positive phrases to myself. These phrases can vary depending on how I'm feeling at the time. They can range from just one word, such as "good", which I'll repeat on the **2** and **4** counts, which are of course the snare drum backbeat. Or I might continually repeat something like "this is easy, this is easy"... One renowned session drummer continually repeats to himself "I can do this... I can do this" if he's experiencing a problem. Ricky Lawson who's worked with Madonna, Phil Collins, Steely Dan and many others) has only one thought in mind when playing something for the first time, it is: "get it right first time!"

The mind can only hold one thought at a time – whether positive or negative. Therefore to replace a negative thought or feeling, a positive phrase (with feeling) needs to be continuously repeated until it drives out the negativity. This is not easy but, with perseverance, does work. Find your personal phrase(s), keep on repeating them and believe in them totally.

This technique is called <u>Positive Affirmation</u> and is not just simply wordplay. Words and thoughts are very powerful and can have dramatic affects – both positive and negative.

Here's a personal example of how the repetition of positive words and thoughts changed my life: For more than half of my life I had an extreme stutter – so bad that when I was a kid, I couldn't get a word out. This was extremely embarrassing and painful for me. Even a simple errand like going to the store and asking for something was a tortuous experience for me.

I now deliver motivational talks and clinics to small and large groups of people. I conduct radio and TV interviews. I teach students in intimate one-on-one lesson formats. So what did I have to do to achieve this? A large part is due to consciously slowing down my speech, giving me more time to think about what I want to say. The other factor was to constantly repeat the following statement to myself, "I am a fluent speaker..." By the term constantly, I don't mean that I walked around all and every day repeating this statement. No, I verbalized and thought this to myself, if and when I felt the need – just like when a sportsman feels the need to employ a sports psychologist. Stuttering was a large part of my life for many, many years and can, at times, rear its ugly head, so I control it by using this method.

to sum up

Focus on what you do well and remember that mistakes are just a part of practicing and playing. This doesn't mean that you should pretend they never occurred and you can make as many as you want... no, just be objective about them and don't let them ruin your playing or a potentially great performance.

'Think' yourself good and in time your mistakes will become rarer and rarer and your good playing will far exceed any bad playing or mistakes – this is the perfect balance.

how to compete by not being competitive

When you announced that you intended to take up the study of drums, enter a drum competition or even move to a big city with the intention of breaking into the big time, was the following comment every thrown at you: "hey, there's a lot of competition out there, doesn't that worry you?"

When I decided to make the break from South Africa and move to one of the world's music capitals, London, I had this comment thrown at me many times. My answer was always, "I don't worry myself about the competition, I only concern myself with what I'm doing". What I meant was that I didn't view other drummers as the competition because if I did, I'd get too bogged down trying to outdo them, resulting in me not keeping my eye on the most important person of all – me!

lengthen your own line

I've studied various martial arts over the years and would like to quote a great story which, although not musical and to some may sound Zen like, perfectly illustrates my thoughts on this whole non-competition theory.

One day a student of lower ranking was sparring against a higher ranking student in a Karate class. To make up for his lack of knowledge and experience, the lower ranked student tried deceptive, tricky maneuvers that were readily countered which, after a short while, resulted in him becoming very flustered and frustrated. In short, he was totally outclassed by his more experienced sparring partner. While all this was happening the chief instructor had been watching and witnessed the less

experienced student get trounced. When the session ended he called over to the demoralized student and invited him into his office.

The instructor took a sheet of paper and a pencil from his desk. He drew a straight line on the paper and posed this question, "how can you make this line shorter?" The student looked at the line and then proceeded to come up with all manner of suggestions such as cutting the line in two with a pair of scissors, folding the page in half, drawing a line or numerous lines through the line in question, rubbing out part of the line, and so on... After the student had exhausted all the possibilities, the instructor picked up the pencil and on the same sheet of paper drew a longer line next to the previous line he had drawn. "Now how does the line look?" he asked. The student immediately replied, "shorter"! "Precisely" said the instructor, "it is always better to create, improve and lengthen your own line of knowledge than to try and cut your opponents line".

Now, applying this philosophy to music, the opponent would of course be another drummer. Therefore, trying to outdo other drummers by being overly concerned with their level of drumming and also attempting to continually show them up is a futile practice. Your efforts would be best directed at improving and lengthening your own line of knowledge and skill. By doing this your eye is then always on the most important person – you. Because it is you and only you, who will get you to where you want to be, not the other drummers that you overly concern yourself with.

I understand and do appreciate that you can't avoid being influenced by other drummers around you – after all you're all going after the same thing, aren't you? So when entering a drumming competition or going for an important audition those other drummers may feel like your competitors – or the competition. So how do you change this attitude?

Simple – use them to your advantage. The secret here is to not continually pit yourself others and try to *outplay* them, but to use what they do and their playing standards as a reference in order for you to measure what you need to do, what changes you need to make and then work out how you're going to get to where you need to be in order to be successful.

the focus is on you!

The truth of the matter is that you can't really outplay anyone. You can only play as well as you can on a given day and within a given situation. In doing this you're not *outplaying* anyone, but simply providing the required level of skill and expertise for the challenge of that particular gig or situation.

So by concentrating all your efforts on your own playing you feel less inclined to compete against others, because the better you become at your art the more self confidence you develop and the less need you have to criticize others. It is only those people who are unsure in what they do and who lack self confidence that feel the need to engage in criticism and *false competition*.

in drum competitions

Young drummers entering any form of drum competition shouldn't concern themselves with what the other candidates are doing. For example: you're in a snare drum competition and waiting in line to play your required part. The drummer in front of you is playing up a real storm and is sounding great. The question now is, do you stop focusing on what you're about to do by letting his playing intimidate you, or do you view his playing as an incentive for you to go out there and play at your utmost best? Hey, I hope it's the second option!

If you chose this option and it still turned out that the drummer in front managed to beat you, then of course you're going to be disappointed. But your outlook then should be that you've gained invaluable experience in that you now have a better understanding of the level required to compete successfully. And the next time you do find yourself in competition, you'll be better prepared, because you will (or should) have raised your standards to stand a better chance of winning.

in auditions

Whenever I've turned up for auditions my attitude has always been that *the best drummer for the job will get the job*. This doesn't mean that I go along with an air of complacency or a couldn't-care-less attitude. No, once again by not concerning myself with how well or how bad the other auditioning drummers might do, I direct all my efforts and focus on how well **I** will do in the task ahead. Thereafter, if I don't get the job, then one or maybe even both of the following things has occurred:

(a) I didn't lengthen my line long enough – maybe due to not preparing myself adequately for the audition, or concentrating on something other than my drumming and the music I was playing.

In fact any other factor attributed to this shortcoming.

(b) I was totally unsuited for the band or artist due to one or maybe even all the following reasons: unsuitable band image; financial considerations; musical incompatibility; contractual obligations; personal differences; or any other factors pertaining to that situation.

These two factors are covered in greater detail in Chapter Seventeen, which deals with how to effectively prepare for auditions.

to sum up

Applied to music, competitiveness and winning is all about developing and realizing as much of your <u>own</u> true potential as you possibly can. It really doesn't matter how someone else is doing. Direct your energies to what you're doing and you'll experience the satisfaction of non-competitive improvement.

how to develop a good reputation

When someone comes When sup to me with a statement like "I never got the break I deserved", my reply is "okay, but can you honestly say that you gave it your total best shot?" In reply the person will usually start becoming very defensive about how unfair everything was for them. Maybe. Good luck can play a part in achieving success and holds a certain amount of validity in getting that big break, but I believe that we, to a large extent, create and control our own luck and lucky breaks.

recommendations

When you look at the reality of drumming and the music business in general, you find that the majority of our work is almost always generated by recommendations from other people (auditions being the other route).

Here's an example: You're playing a gig one night and things are real slooooowww. The club is empty and you're playing to an audience of just five people. The other musicians in the band are demoralized and generally just going through the motions. They keep glancing at their watches wishing that the set was over and that they were off stage. But not you – you're not holding back. Even though the audience numbers are pretty sad, you're still giving it everything you've got and are playing up a real storm. Now without you realizing it, one of those five people in the audience just happens to be a keyboard player and a good friend of another band. This band is one you've have

heard of but have never met and they're on the look out for a new drummer, because their present one, although a good player, is very unreliable and has let them down one time too many. The band has just signed a major Indie record deal, recorded their first album and is off on a support tour soon. But before things can really take off the management company has said that they need to sort out their drummer situation immediately. They also haven't yet started advertising for a new drummer, so no one knows that they are looking. I guess you could say this band has a whole lot more going for it than the less than enthusiastic outfit that you're currently drumming with?

So you finish your set and leave the stage. The keyboard player approaches and compliments you, stating how impressed he was with the positive attack in your playing even though the club is virtually empty. He then proceeds to tell you about this band and asks if you'd be interested in auditioning. Wow... you can hardly believe your luck and just about maintain an air of coolness replying that you're definitely interested in the job. "Cool" he replies and says he'll personally recommend you for the job, because he thinks you're just the kind of drummer they need.

Two weeks later after a successful audition, you find yourself in another band and rehearsing extensively for the forthcoming tour. You've also been put on a basic retainer which means that you now have regular money in your pocket and can cover the rent with no hassle. And how about this, you've even managed to get your face onto the cover of the album because the record company hadn't yet sent it off to be printed.

So... things are looking up and the future looks rosy. How did this come about? Was it luck? Partly. The luck part of it was only due to the dude being in the club at the time. Everything else was down to <u>your own efforts</u> because you initiated the whole thing by playing to your full potential that night and didn't hold back on yourself. Do you think that keyboard player would have approached you had you been dejectedly going through the motions – like your fellow band members? I don't think so. The impression you gave at that gig is what influenced his decision to approach and then recommend you for the job. If you had projected a *switched-off* attitude you wouldn't have attracted his attention and wouldn't have created that *lucky break*. Makes simple sense doesn't it?

a good reputation attracts lucky breaks

Because of practicing right; being well prepared for rehearsals and performances; showing up on time; playing enthusiastically with a good attitude; projecting a professional image at all times; you encourage people to have confidence in you and your abilities. As a result this develops that *good* reputation which puts the message out that you're able to take care of business and starts attracting the lucky breaks to you – time after time.

to sum up

So when people say "what a great drummer, but it's sad how he never managed to get that lucky break", I'm inclined to believe that the breaks were there waiting to be taken, but somehow, something held this drummer back, and that something is usually the drummer's own self limiting attitude.

how to make the most of your full potential

Some of the most consistent questions I get asked by prospective students, are:
- How long will it take me to play well?
- How long did it take you to reach your level of playing?
- When will I be good enough to play in a band?

It's up to you

Everything starts (and ends) with you, in that...
- You choose to take up the drums
- You decide how good you want to be
- You decide how much time and effort you're willing to put into practice
- You decide how good you are going to be by pushing or limiting your progress
- You choose what to do and where to be in order to attract the breaks

...which in the long term determines how successful you will be in your musical career.

Every individual has different levels of awareness, discipline, enthusiasm, social skills, motivation, natural talent, desire – in fact any element needed to enable them to reach their desired standard of playing. And then in addition, what level of financial achievement they aspire to achieve.

As previously pointed out, I believe that any musician who engages in diligent daily practice determines his or her own rate of progress. A key factor in stunting this progress would be if

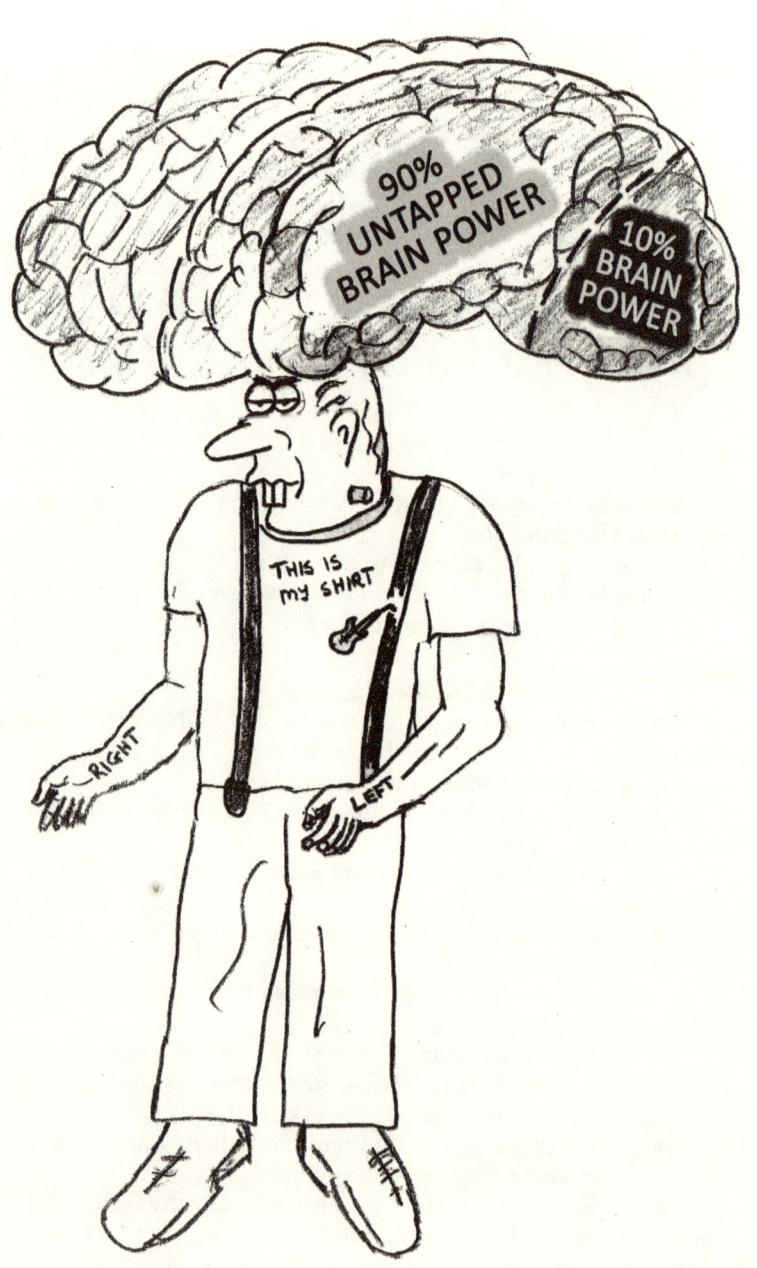

he or she mentally holds themselves back. Drummers can hold themselves back by mentally telling themselves that they are incapable of reaching a certain standard or level of performance. This is totally negative and a drawback because deep down, most of us know that we are capable of achieving a whole lot more than we presently have or are. On the other hand it's also sensible practice and a sign of maturity to admit to your shortcomings. Therefore, it's a case of striking a balance between these two attitudes and making it work for you.

positive mental reserves

If psychologists tell us that we use only 10% of our brainpower (some say even less), then it stands to reason that we have an unbelievably huge reservoir of untapped brainpower to draw on. So, if we find that we're not achieving optimum results, then I believe it's because we aren't taking advantage of this rich reserve of positive energy and are limiting ourselves by holding back on our full potential.

to sum up

Your potential for improvement is unlimited if over a long period of time you are willing to sensibly practice and study with consistency.

how to increase your powers of observation and listening

Often when teaching, I've asked students to repeat a rudiment or exercise I've demonstrated. It's amazing how many of them don't realize that what they repeat isn't the same as I've just shown them. Sometimes this is due to inexperience, especially in the case of the beginner, but when the same thing happens with a more experienced drummer, the problem is more than likely due to a lack of observation and effective listening.

the three 'S's

Acute observation and awareness are abilities which all gifted drummers possess. This reminds me of an article I read in a British drumming magazine that featured Dave Weckl. The journalist asked Dave what he considered to be his strong points, he replied "a high degree of awareness".

I have a concept and method of raising self awareness that I personally use and also teach to all of my students. It works fantastically well and I call it the Three 'S's approach.

Sight – are you making a <u>visual study</u> of yourself as you play?

Sound – how closely are you really <u>listening</u> to yourself?

Sensation – are you aware of <u>how you feel</u> while you play?

You can effectively use the Three 'S's approach no matter what style of drumming you're into and no matter what skill level you're currently at. The three 'S's approach will become very apparent as you read through this chapter and learn how to effectively apply it to your practice and performance agenda.

using a recording

Instead of just bashing away and fantasizing that you sound like your favorite drummer, learn to listen more closely and find out whether what you're playing is coming out precisely the way you want it to sound. The most effective means to achieve this is to record yourself and then listen back and judge your performance. Often, what you hear will not be what you expected.

For example: After having recorded something you thought was badly played, you may be pleasantly surprised to hear that it's actually very good and sounds just the way you intended to hear it. Unfortunately, the other side of this coin is when you've played something believing it to be really cool, and then on listening back find it sucks and sounds nothing like you thought it would. While the first result is always cool, this latter experience can be pretty disheartening.

Many drummers are wary of recording themselves as this tends to show up mistakes and shortcomings. This really shouldn't be viewed in such a manner because these recordings are an essential tool to improving and serve as a personal reference regarding standard and achievement.

your undivided attention

Another advantage of recording yourself is the opportunity it gives to go back and identify mistakes you knew you had made, but couldn't pick out while physically playing. This is because when engaged in only one activity such as listening, you listen more acutely and are better able to zone in where and why these mistakes occurred. In other words, your focus is not divided between playing and listening, but all your problem solving attention is focused only on what you're listening to.

In regard to this: experienced drummers have agreed, when quizzed about certain aspects of a solo they've just played, that they usually can't analyze what they've played – unless the solo was heavily structured or maybe even charted out. This is because while playing, their concentration is geared up more for physical execution and creative flow, rather than objective listening. They may be able to recall a problem area (if one was encountered), but whether they will be able to identify why they went wrong is up to how much objective listening was being used at the time.

In light of the above, it is possible to identify mistakes

using objective listening when physically playing, however you should realize that this is something that is a developed skill and takes much practice. It will only work following a lot of time in the study, practice and performance of drumming.

Here are various suggestions to improve your awareness in many areas of drumming:

When listening back to...

Rudiments (single surface practice) – Is the performance smooth and are the notes evenly spaced? Is the articulation correct? Are the accented notes loud enough? Are you missing any intended rim shots? Does your long roll sound evenly *closed*, or is one hand louder? Is your single stroke roll consistently even? Is your left hand flam as clear and precise as your right, or vice versa? Do the unaccented notes in your accented triplet have the correct spacing between the accented notes? Are you steady when practicing all the above to a metronome? And so on...

Aside from focused listening, are you observing what you're doing by using a mirror? For example: Are your wrist strokes controlled or are you using excessive forearm movement? If you're using forearm strokes as in Moeller method, is the motion relaxed and flowing? Are your sticks uniform in height when playing alternate strokes? What about your actual grip – are your hands in a natural position and the fingers in control of the sticks, or is there too much tension in your forearms due to a much too tight grip? Do your shoulders rise and fill with tension when changing from slow patterns to faster figures? And so on...

On the drum set – While practicing grooves are you really as *in the pocket* with the click as you think you are? If you're attempting to play a lazy behind-the-beat half-time shuffle, are you grooving or *dragging*? Does your standard jazz ride pattern truly have that *swinging* triplet feel? Can you play those lightning fast double bass patterns at half the tempo, and is so how consistent do they sound? Are your linear triplet based patterns between hand and feet (RLB RLB etc) powerfully consistent? Are your fills in time or are you speeding up or slowing down (probably one of the most consistent complaints about drummers from other musicians), and so on...

Reading – Record yourself while practicing your reading material, then listen back and observe carefully. Are you playing exactly what is printed on the page? Have you missed any dynamic markings? Is the spacing of the rests between the played notes correct or rushed? Did you miss any accents? Are your closed rolls crisp or sloppy? What else did you observe?

Try this exercise to improve your reading ability. Without even picking up your sticks, <u>only read</u> through the material at first. Treat this the same way as when reading a book containing words and read as slow as required in order to <u>take in everything</u> on the page – don't let anything slip by. In doing this you bring all of your observation powers into play and when you can fluently read what is on paper, you'll find that reading and playing simultaneously will be a whole lot easier.

Additionally, if there is a required tempo marking then make sure you can play everything (without mistakes) at a slower tempo, before attempting to play at the prescribed tempo. I have found the best way to achieve this is to notch up the tempo in degrees of three (i.e. 65bpm and then to 68bpm, etc). By doing this you hardly notice this increase in speed and retain the information easier as you work toward the desired tempo.

If you're practicing a chart which you'll eventually play to a music-minus-drums track or CD track; only once you've read through the chart and are comfortable with the *dots* and have (slowly) worked out the physical execution of the more difficult parts or patterns; attempt the whole chart. Then depending on tempo, increase this until you are able to play at the prescribed tempo. After all this, if you have the technology, then record yourself and listen back and acknowledge the improvement or take note of what needs work for you to eventually play the track as it should sound.

using a drum machine

If you possess a digital drum machine or computer based sequencing software program, then use this to improve your drumming by trying the following: In real-time, *play* into the machine the material you're working on, whether it be rudiments, beats, fills or reading exercises. If it's a difficult groove then play the individual patterns in one at a time, until you have the complete part in the machine. If it's a snare drum chart that's very quick then slow down the click and utilize Extra Slow Playing. If you find it difficult to play your exercise even at an Extra Slow Playing tempo, then program it in Step write mode. Once you've entered your material into the machine then set the tempo to a comfortable level for practice purposes.

If appropriate you can loop the data you entered and play along without any breaks over and over. If you've programmed a reading exercise into your machine then approach it in the same way as described earlier in how to improve your reading. Once you are comfortable playing along to the machine then you can record yourself and once again listen and observe closely.

build your personal recorded collection

I have recordings of myself engaged in practice going back many years. This is my personal recorded collection and is as prized as photo albums and scrapbooks. I always find it interesting to listen back to this material and hear how my drumming has developed and changed over the years. Aside from these practice recordings, I also have recordings made at gigs with various bands. These do however tend to point to the early years in my playing career as I later progressed to recording proper studio albums which I can also listen back to and assess how my drumming and musicality has evolved.

You can do the same no matter where you presently are in your career. Begin the process by building up your own personal recordings in the same manner I've described and you will start to focus more closely on where your drumming is now, and where you want it to go.

to sum up

Most of us do pay attention to whatever we're playing and working on, and drummers with especially greater powers of observation and listening have no problem there. But should you feel that you're lacking in these areas, then I believe that by implementing the suggestions put forward in this chapter, you will greatly benefit by developing these important faculties.

practising and playing to recorded music

I find it worrying when drummers who have little or no experience of playing with other musicians, keep religiously going for lessons but put little effort into finding a band to play with. I do appreciate that finding a suitable band can often prove difficult as all the necessary factors need to fall into place. If this is the case, then I suggest the next best thing – practice playing along to recorded music that preferably has no drums on the recording.

For the less experienced drummer this form of practice can be viewed as *pre-rehearsal*, in that it gives an insight to what it will be like to play with other musicians. It develops what I call the *performance head*. The attitude required when playing along to music as opposed to merely dry (no music) drum exercise material.

When practicing dry exercises you have the luxury of stopping anytime to examine where and why you went wrong. Try doing the same thing in a practical grade examination or on a live show and see what reaction you get! If you aren't fired on the spot the band will certainly think you've gone insane!

developing an attitude of continuity

In my teaching I encourage all my students to get used to the idea of <u>playing through mistakes</u>. By this I don't imply that they should simply ignore the mistakes and pretend they never happened. No, they should attempt to play through them and then sort them out <u>after</u> they've played the exercise or song through to the end. This approach gives their playing and more importantly their attitude to playing, a feeling of continuity by developing the stamina, concentration and coordination to finish what they started – mistakes or no mistakes. If this attitude is not taken on board you will never be able to play through a whole evening's performance, let alone something as short as a four bar phrase, if you're used to continually stopping and starting while playing.

and it's not just for beginners!

To ensure maximum performance, professional athletes have to keep their physical as well as their mental muscles in peak condition to ensure they perform at their best. It's no different for musicians.

I remember back to when I had a layoff from live performance for a period of nine months. When I started touring again, I found that my concentration and stamina had greatly deteriorated and after every gig was physically and mentally drained. To remedy this, I devoted time to practicing long endurance exercises (without stopping) to build up stamina and also played along to recorded music to develop my *performance head*. After a short time I found myself regaining those lost facilities needed to play effectively. This is a good example of the 'if-you-don't-use-it-you-lost-it' syndrome.

the way to do it

For drum set practice you're going to need a good set of headphones. I recommend the closed type that fully covers your ears, thereby cutting out excess outside volume or in ear monitors. The more airy, ambient type of headphones that lightly press against your ear aren't suitable because they allow too much outside volume in, which makes it difficult to hear and keep time to the recorded music. However, if you're using a practice pad set or a padded out drum set then these headphones are fine, because they allow the low volume of the pads to filter through giving you a reference of how and what you're physically playing.

At first, choose songs that are not too demanding and which you'll find relatively easy to play from beginning to end. If you don't have any music-minus-drums type tracks that usually have a count-in bar, then you'll have to pick up the groove of the song as soon as you can. You may want to turn up the bass frequency and reduce the treble in order to make it easier to lock in with the bass guitar.

If you've chosen regular CD tracks then you'll be playing along to music that already has a recorded drum track. This is handy because the existing drum track serves three purposes:

(1) The existing track can be regarded as a metronome (click) to play along with to keep you in time;

(2) The recorded drum track is a reference as to what you should be playing beat-wise and also teaches you where to place your fills;

(3) When playing to music rather than just a metronome you think about the feel and groove of the song. Therefore, your drumming develops musically and not just rhythmically.

Should a song you've chosen have a difficult fill that you just can't seem to work out, then play the closest approximation you can come up with. You'll probably find that after repeated listening and playing, the correct fill could just fall into place. The same applies to a difficult beat in that after spending some time playing your closest approximation, the correct rhythm can often just *appear*. If this doesn't happen then seek out the help and advice of an experienced drummer or teacher. Additionally, if you have the luxury of a vari-speed playback system then slow down the track and listen to the difficult beat or fill. This can often make it much easier to identify what is being played.

Supply the groove

Available on the market are various music-minus-drums packages in different formats from CD to MP3 downloads to DVD. This is where the drums have been left out of the music and the object is to play along to these 'empty' tracks and supply the groove. Depending on which package you buy the recorded material may have a click running throughout to play along with, or just a count-in with no click supplied. Both are recommended.

Some packages have sample recordings of what the drum track should sound like and may also include drum charts enabling you to read the part. I cannot stress enough the importance of using this kind of drum workout, particularly if you have little or no experience playing with a band. This method of practice will never take the place of playing with real musicians but nonetheless is an excellent substitute to hone

your play-along skills.

For the more experienced drummer not working with a band, this is valuable practice as it helps keep alive the *performance head*. Aside from this reason you can also experiment by playing to music in unfamiliar styles. This will cause you to stretch musically and expand your repertoire of styles. This of course applies to any drummer, whether in a band or not. These music-minus-drums packages are available from all good drum stores and also via the internet. If you've never used any then check them out because they really are useful tools in developing and improving your drumming.

Remember also that playing to recorded music can greatly increase your chances for an audition should your prospective band have a CD available. You can prepare yourself beforehand by playing along to their material, viewing this as a *pre-audition*. This subject is covered in greater detail in Chapter Seventeen.

Make up your personal repertoire

For the less experienced drummer, once you're comfortable playing to recorded music one song at a time, you may want to record a few numbers one after the other. This serves as your personal repertoire or set-list. I suggest you make your first set of songs approximately 30 minutes in length. In time and as your concentration span and stamina increases, you'll be able to expand the duration of your set. As you gain more experience, you should progressively increase the standard of playing required in your repertoire from easy to difficult. If you want to develop your reading and notation skills then try writing out charts for the material.

When you are able to play uninterrupted for an hour or so, your concentration and stamina will be top notch. And when the time comes for you to join a band, you'll have a more than better chance of keeping up with the performance requirements.

While on this subject I'd like to relate a short story about a drummer called Chris Cooper who at the time was one of my students. With several years playing experience, Chris was a professional drummer in a signed UK band that regularly undertook British, European and American tours. As he tended to play the same music all the time he was inspired to put the advice offered here into practice after reading this chapter.

Being a huge Beatles and Ringo fan he decided (for the fun of it) to put together a Beatles set and play along. He told me he really enjoyed himself because it caused him to play differently from the way he normally plays with his band. Here you see a good example that playing to recorded music is not just reserved for beginners and the inexperienced, but for all levels of drummer.

record yourself

As discussed in the previous chapter on recording your drumming, a useful tip is to record yourself while you play along to these packages. Obvious methods are to use some kind of digital recorder or computer recording software – some mini recorders also have this feature. You really want to try and use a machine that has stereo inputs because the intention is to record the pre-recorded music on one channel and your drums on the other channel. This means when playing back you have the advantage of utilizing the balance control to listen to your drum track with or without the pre-recorded music on the other channel.

get creative

If you don't have any of these packages then an interesting substitute is to go through your music collection and dig out songs that don't feature any drums on the recording. Usually, these types of songs are in a softer, more acoustic kind of format.

It may at first seem strange and feel very odd playing along to this kind of track, but the more you do it, the more you'll realize just how closely it forces you to listen to what is happening musically within the song. You'll discover that you'll automatically be expanding your listening skills and developing a much keener musical ear. In a sense when doing this, you're also learning how to construct your own drum part. Try it – its great fun.

to sum up

The information offered in this chapter really does work and is an excellent means for the less experienced drummer to gain pre-band experience. For the more experienced player you can have fun in playing to different styles and let your drumming develop in other directions.

Lastly, remember to always respect copyright restrictions on any previously recorded material and to use this form of re-recording solely for your own use and benefit.

drummers are real musicians

How many of the following comments have you heard or been subjected to?
- "there are four musicians and a drummer in the band"
- "drummers aren't real musicians"
- "drummers make noise, not music"
- "will the drummer keep quiet while we're tuning up?" (ignoring the fact that the drummer may also be also tuning up)
- "you mean you actually have musical notation for the drums?"
- "will the toy department keep quiet please" (remark passed to the percussion section of a military band)
- "he just keeps the beat" (comment made by a guitarist about my drumming just after I had finished playing a set featuring a drum solo)
- "it's okay, we'll put the amps in front of the drums" (this really happened at a gig I played on a small stage!)
- "the drummer is always too loud" (obviously a comment made by someone who has never played with guitarists)

Ah yes... I could go on and on and I'm sure you could add a few remarks you've been subjected to or heard directed at other drummers.

Welcome to the grudge chapter! Yep, this is the section of the book where I release and get out into the open all my frustrations of what it has been like and still is, to bear the brunt of those hilarious drummer jokes. And I know I'm not alone when expressing this...

Okay, before I get branded a wet rag by taking things too seriously, I'd like to point out that just like anybody else, I love to laugh and consider myself to have a pretty good sense of humor. But I have to admit that after a while a lot of these snide, dumb comments directed toward us drummers starts to wear thin. Interestingly, have you ever noticed how other musicians react if you turn the tables on them? What's that old saying: when the shoe is on the other foot... I'm cool with the whole drummer joke thing, what really gets my blood boiling is that ignorant attitude which regards drummers as lesser or non-musicians, and also that what we do on our instruments is not considered music but noise. I don't know about you, but I find that comment pretty offensive!

We DO make music!!

The drum is not considered to be a melodic instrument and in essence I have to agree, because, if you play a snare or any other drum by itself it produces only one pitch – the exceptions are drums where the pitch can be altered. The pitch of timpani for example can be raised or lowered by a foot pedal that tightens and slackens the drumhead. Another melodic drum is the African Talking Drum which features tension ropes that allow pitch shifting. Held in position under one arm and played with a special beater with the other hand, the pitch is shifted by squeezing the drum thereby loosening the head.

Now without getting too technical, I'd like to add that to a certain extent it is possible to change the pitch on conventional drums such as toms. The easiest method is by pressing down on the drumhead with one hand or stick, while you play with the other. This pressure on the head lifts the pitch giving you a small range of notes to construct a *melody*. Tone shifting is also possible by playing on different areas of the drumhead surface – play to the outside of the head near the rim and you get a softer, thinner sound. Move to the centre and the result is a thicker and much louder sound. Now put together a whole drum set where each drum is tuned to a different note (pitch and note have pretty much the same meaning) and using the above methods you have the scope to come up with a certain degree of *melodic* composition.

For great examples of this type of drumming listen to Johnny Rabb, Steve Smith and Jack de Johnette – to name but a few. The tones and nuances these drummers extract from their

instruments is amazing and to my ears sounds extremely melodic. In ensemble situations their playing, aside from being rhythmic, is also very musical and their drum solos have melodies with form and structure. Maybe the real musicians haven't been listening close enough or don't understand this concept? What about Santana's percussion? I hear melodies within their ensemble playing. Listen to a Neil Peart drum solo and what you're hearing is *percussive melody*.

they start young

Discouraging, uninformed comments can start at an early age for young people when expressing a desire to play the drums. Typical comments are "Oh no, not the drums, why don't you take up a proper instrument?" or, *"no, drums make too much noise"*. Then there's, *"no, drums take up too much space"*, and so on...

Thankfully not all parents are like this and in my teaching career have met many who are very supportive of their kid's drumming aspirations. But it has to be said that many people do have this picture of drums being just too big and too loud. Okay, it's true, drums are loud. But that's also what's so cool about them. And for sure, a beginner could drive anyone round the bend thrashing about with no rhythm, and yes... a full set can take up a bit of space. But that's the nature of the instrument! As to the noise factor: have you ever heard a novice piano player? Aaaaagh.

So let's compromise as everyone has to start somewhere, which is at the beginning – and solutions can be agreed concerning practice times and the volume aspect. Nowadays there are a multitude of products on the market enabling drummers to practice at all volume levels in virtually any situation. Electronic kits, single practice pads, full practice sets and dampening pads that fit over conventional drums and cymbals allow practicing to take place in even noise restricted areas. I agree that you don't get the same feel and response as you would in playing an un-dampened acoustic drum set, but hey, if you're keen you'll still get the work done and keep on moving ahead by always improving. If I think back to all the hours spent in practice I can safely say that pad practice far outweighs the time spent on real drums.

other instruments make noise too!

Drums and percussion are not the only instruments

that can be offensive to the ears. As I said before, ever heard an inexperienced student practicing violin? All the cats in the vicinity invite themselves around to join in this agony on the ears. What about a beginner on saxophone? honk... squeak... blat That'll ensure all the geese and ducks in the neighborhood arrive to investigate the mating calls. Even though the piano can bring about tears of joy, try listening to 1 or 2 hours of solid scales by a beginner and those tears are of pain! I say this as I recall living in an apartment and being woken up early on Sunday mornings (after a late night's gig) by the sound of a nine-year-old girl merrily plonking away on an out of tune piano. No, she wasn't next door, she was one floor up at the far end of the passage and we could still hear her! Not being one to discourage any form of musical aspiration, as fellow musicians we came to a compromise as to when she would do her plonking and I kindly showed her where the dampening pedal was on her instrument. So we were both happy – she got her practice I and I got my much-needed beauty sleep. Ha!

drums are equal in stature

The piano, which incidentally is a percussion instrument because you have to *strike* the keys to produce a sound, is my favorite *melodic* instrument. Listening to this being played skillfully can be a beautiful experience. But hey, the same applies to drums and in some ways even more so.

I remember back to when I was 14 years old and went to a jazz concert with my older sister and her boyfriend. Even though at that time I didn't understand the music I was totally mesmerized by the drummer. His playing flowed so effortlessly with the rest of the band and when he took a solo, played in what I now recognize and would call Max Roach style drumming. Man what a player. I only wish I could remember who he was. All I can remember is the audience going wild for this black drummer who was probably in his 40's, a tad on the overweight side, smiling continuously and in complete command of the music and his instrument. Beautiful!

A good drummer can transfix his audience when playing a drum solo because it's not just the music of the solo that excites them, but also the powerful visual impact of the drummers playing. Drums come from the soul and that beat comes from the heart. Consider the musical and visual impact of solos by the following drummers who are all very different to each other: Steve

Smith, Carl Palmer, Tommy Lee, Joey Jordison, Dom Famularo, Virgil Donati, etc...

So the drums, while maybe not being the most sociable of instruments such as an acoustic guitar played round the campfire (although at the beginning of time and still in certain cultures today drums are a primary means of communication and music), have equal entertainment stature and value when played correctly and in the right environment.

'real' musicians

Man, this is cool... ever onwards with my grudge chapter. We move on to two main bodies of individuals who, I believe, are the chief throwers of drummer ridicule. The first are you singers out there! As always I'll mention that there are exceptions to the rule because I've worked with some great singers who were an absolute treat. Unfortunately, I can pretty much count them on one hand, (oh, alright... two hands) and with only a few exceptions most of these also played a musical instrument.

Now this doesn't mean that singers who don't play an instrument aren't cool to work with. But the reality is that most who stand there looking pretty (or cool) soaking up the limelight, wouldn't know how to spell the word rhythm if it hit them in the face, let alone trying to implement it into their singing. Then there are those who understand and appreciate that they need musical backing to help them look and sound good, but have no idea how vital each instrument is, or how individual instruments fit together to create that sound which backs up their songs. As a result they feel the need to tell drummers how to play, when really they don't have a clue what they're talking about. My apologies if I have offended anyone, but please remember that these are purely my personal feelings on the subject. But hey, what the hell, while we're on the subject here's a good singer joke for you:

Question: How can you tell when there's a singer knocking at your door?

Answer: Easy, they never know when to come in!

Admittedly and quite rightly, there are times when drummers deserve all the flak they get, if they fail to take care of business efficiently. But, if a drummer is competent and doing his job correctly, there should be no problem right? Well, not quite... I've had the experience of being told by a singer to change something I'd been playing (something the band and I knew to be right) to something that was completely wrong. Fortunately the situation worked out fine because once I'd played the wrong part a few times; we went back to the original part. You guessed it – at the singer's request, after he realized how stupid the new part sounded!

So, come on you singers out there, we really do understand that it's your reputation on the line whenever you're up there performing, but it's ours too – so give us a little credit and stick to what you do best and leave the drumming to drummers – after all, we're trying our best to make everyone sound good!

And now, ladies and gentlemen, for your reading pleasure we move on to the second body of *drummer abuse throwers* – *guitarists*. In particular *lead* guitarists. Ah yes, a can of hairspray, a spotlight, an amp that can be cranked to volume 11 and most guitarists are in seventh heaven. Naturally again, there are always the exceptions. I've worked with some excellent, very down to earth guitarists who not only had the melodic side of their instrument sown up, but were also blessed with a superb sense of time and rhythm. However, in my observations I have to say that many guitarists' sense of time is up the spout. They spend so much energy focusing on playing 1000 notes a minute that somewhere along the line taste and melody is sacrificed. Sorry guitarists, but once again do please remember that this is merely my personal opinion. In any case, and if you haven't already done so, then maybe it's time to have a word with the drummer in your band to see if he feels the same way. Incidentally, as this is the second edition of this book, I've had contact with a lot of drummers who read the first edition and voted this as one of their favorite chapters!

I have a guitarist friend called Jojo who in the mid 80's emigrated from South Africa to the US and now lives in Los Angeles. He left with the reputation of being one of the finest players to ever come out of South Africa. He has awesome technique, excellent creative song-writing skills and possesses great sense of time. He plays in this manner because he took the time and effort to develop and be this way. He's a cool dude and I have a great respect for him as a musician and as a person, and enjoyed playing with him in two bands. So you see I'm not biased and give respect and praise where due. Jo is the same; he has a genuine respect for good drummers with one of his favorites being Rod Morgenstein. Now, if only those other guitarists would do the same and appreciate what a good drummer is all about, life would be so less complicated!

stand up for your rights!

It's unfortunate that we drummers also tend to take the flak a lot of the time for the mistakes pertaining to time and tempo. If the song slows down or speeds up it's usually considered to be just the drummer who is the offender in this situation. Now if it is the drummer at fault then I don't stand up to defend him or her because they aren't doing their job and I suggest they head for the practice room. But what if it's not the drummer at fault? Rarely is it contemplated that maybe the bass player is dragging so much that the drummer has to compensate by slowing down to work with the bass to make the song sit better. Or maybe the guitarist is so stiff in his rhythm playing that when the singer requests the drummer to pick up the tempo, the drummer gets blamed for not being able to implement the request because the guitarist's unyielding strum just won't allow it.

As drummers I agree that it is our prime responsibility to lay down good time. But if there is a time or tempo discrepancy, it might just be another musician in the band because after all, we aren't the only ones laying down time and creating rhythm, right? So if you do get the blame for something you <u>know</u> is not your fault, then stand up for your rights as a drummer and don't blindly accept these criticisms and accusations.

Just because we're classified as the timekeepers doesn't mean that mistakes in this area are always our fault.

to sum up

I hope you enjoyed this chapter. While it's meant to be taken seriously, in the same breath it is also a bit tongue in cheek, as there are many variables which come into play when interacting and performing with other musicians. I don't really hate singers or guitarists; I just don't like the ignorant ones who make our jobs a lot tougher to do. Yes, I do find a lot of drummer jokes funny and can laugh at myself. But fun is fun and work is work. So in this light, let other musicians know you are a <u>real musician</u> and that what you play on your drums is <u>music</u> and not noise!

And lastly, there is a well known and oh so true statement – *A band is only ever as good as it's drummer.* Nuff said!

how to successfully prepare for auditions

In 1984 I went for my first major British audition. This was for an English rock band that had just supported Van Halen on a stadium tour of the US. Performing in front of 30,000 people per show on average, they had just released their second album and were doing very well. Before proceeding further, I will point out that prior to this audition I had tasted a reasonable amount of success in Africa while working with two top recording bands. But I refer to this audition as my first major break as this was a chance for me to step into a bigger international music scene.

Back to the band... While on the Stateside tour the drummer and keyboard player announced they would be leaving once they returned to England. The reason being that neither enjoyed the constant traveling and being away from home for such long periods. So, seeing the ad in a national music newspaper that read *'Drummer wanted for rock band with major record deal'*, I decided to apply for the job. I called the number and spoke to the management company's secretary who said that initially my details would be passed on to the band and should I be requested to attend auditions, I'd receive a phone call giving details of when and where they would take place. Now this was exciting stuff because I'd never applied for an audition of such magnitude before.... so I waited anxiously. Sound familiar?

A few days later I got the call and was requested to go along to the band's record company's office in Camden Town, London. I was told this first meeting would only be an interview with the selected applicants going on to a short list for the first audition, and then a final audition.

Having a few days in hand before the interview I decided to fully prepare myself by buying a copy of the band's new album. I listened and played to all of the songs, totally familiarizing myself with their music. The day before the interview I played my final *rehearsal*, satisfying myself that I could play all of the material well and also that I would appear knowledgeable in being able to quote song titles and discuss the music.

Setting off early the next day I arrived in good time and was told by the receptionist to go through to an adjoining room where the band would shortly call for me. Entering the room I noticed three other drummers present. I nodded a greeting and sat down to wait. Nobody spoke.

From behind a closed door I could hear the faint sound of music and wondered how the present auditioning drummer was doing. After a few minutes the door opened, out he came and left the way I had come in. The door closed and all was quiet again. A few minutes later the next drummer was called in and again we waited.

At this point another drummer arrived. Now I'll always remember this dude because he walked into the room as though he owned the building and had already got the job. Dressed in his best denims and leather and sporting a pair of designer sunglasses (although typically for UK weather, it was heavily overcast and raining outside), he strutted around hands on hips, chewing gum and looking all of us over with a 'you haven't got a chance' attitude. Eventually, in went the next drummer and again we waited. By now Mr Wonderful had sat down, switched on his Walkman (now an iPod) and was demonstrating to us how good he was by tapping away to music on his thigh with a pair of sticks.

At last it was my turn. I nervously walked through the door into an office immediately recognizing the singer and bass guitarist from the cover of the album I had bought (incidentally, I had bought a now antiquated analog cassette tape album of the band – ahhh the good old days). After exchanging greetings we immediately got down to business with them saying that they were pressed for time as they had approximately 30 drummers to see that day. So, at their request I handed over a tape that featured me playing on three rock songs with one of my previous bands.

They listened, smiled, giving the indication that they

liked what they were hearing. They gave each track around a one-minute listen. I had another tape with me onto which I'd recorded a solo and asked if they'd like to hear this. "Yes" they replied as they were keen to hear my technical abilities. I was excited now and on a roll, because I knew the solo was good and thought "this'll impress them".

Lesson number one: Never present a recording of a solo that takes more than 10 seconds to get to what you want to showcase! Unfortunately for me, I'd started off the solo with sparse atmospheric ideas. A great idea when you're on stage with a captive audience and have the time in which to do this. But when you're in a situation where time is very limited then a *mood building* solo (as I call it), just doesn't get a fair listening. I was under the naïve impression that they would give time to listen to the whole solo and appreciate the compositional way in which it had been structured – but we never got that far. My tape was around 8 minutes long! The last section of the solo was great in featuring impressive classic rock solo ingredients such as fast triplet patterns between hands and feet, a quick ostinato (continuous) bass drum with polyrhythmic figures and fast paradiddle type flurries around the set. This is of course where I should have cued the tape from. You can imagine the shock when my drum solo tape was ejected in less than a minute! I was left spluttering and muttering, "er, it gets better... and faster." Half smiling they handed my tape back to me.

They followed this *disaster* with a question asking what I thought of their departing drummer's playing on their last album. Instead of saying what I thought, which was that he was really good and suited the band well, I was now no longer myself and had sort of lost the plot. With a nervous laugh and air of false self-confidence I replied that his drumming was "okay".

Lesson number two: Bearing in mind I thought the previous drummer was a lot more than *okay*, my reply implied that I could do a better job – and that he had not. Now I must stress that you should never knock or criticize a departing member of a band or show, as he or she may be leaving on amicable terms and you could easily offend the remaining members. In fact, the outgoing drummer may even be a brother or sister of one of the band. In my case, although I hadn't directly criticized the leaving drummer, I had unwittingly implied by my attitude that I did not think he was adequate and that I without question was better. What I had wanted to say was that their drummer was cool and although my style was different, if given the opportunity to join the band I would do my best to play the music with my own personal touch, without detracting from the band's original sound and identity. Unfortunately, it never quite came out like that. I do believe the reason for this was due to my unsettling shock at seeing them eject my solo tape so early, and then putting up a barrier of false self confidence which resulted in me not being myself anymore.

Naturally I never got the job. Had I handled the interview more wisely and then gone on to physically audition, I'm positive that I would have had a good chance of getting the job, or at the very least, been short-listed for the final audition. You do, as they say, learn by your mistakes. So, I bombed out on my first major break. But incidentally, Mr Wonderful with all his cool attitude and slick leather never got the job either! I guess he was maybe just too cool for this pretty down to earth band? We'll never know.

this time it worked

A few weeks later I auditioned (without interview) for another band that played original jazz/rock material. This time I got the job the same day. Being more of a part time unit the band was not a huge financial earner, but comprised some of London's top session players. So from that angle it was a good situation to be in.

Having no prior knowledge of the band's material I turned up and was auditioned by only the keyboard player, who also happened to be the band leader. After setting up my drums he gave me the drum charts of the music I was to play. This was a bit of a shock because at the time I wasn't the best sight-reader in the world. Without panic I adopted the attitude described in Chapter Ten when I was required to play the 'On The Track' xylophone piece. It worked again!

I got the job partly through being able to read to a passable standard and also by keeping my ears open and busking some of the more unreadable parts. While I was playing I knew that there were moments where I'd lost my place on the charts, but my positive attack on playing just seemed to get me through these sticky bits. So even though I never made a lot of money with this band, I enjoyed the high quality musicianship and the venues we played. I made a lot of good contacts, in other words networked, and learned a great deal more about the London music scene.

unsuccessful audition factors

Attending audition after audition can sometimes be very demoralizing if you let this break down your confidence. Just remember, if you don't get a job you've auditioned for it could be due to one of many factors that have nothing to do with your playing. Some of these reasons may be:
- your image doesn't fit the image of the band or show
- there could be an age limit meaning you may be too old or too young
- there may be a clash of personalities
- your commitment and ties may be viewed as unsuitable – perhaps you have a day job or are married and can't travel freely, need a guaranteed amount of money to survive each month or you have to give your present band sufficient notice before you can leave
- your playing may be up to standard but doesn't suit the band's style of music

audition tips

To ensure that you give yourself a more than fighting chance of success when auditioning, I present to you the following advice. It's for you to decide whether you use all or only some of the points listed to give yourself the very best chance you can on the day.

1. Try to make sure that the band you are auditioning for is <u>sympathetic</u> to your style of drumming and that they, in turn, play your preferred style of music. On one occasion I answered an ad requiring a jazz drummer and on arriving at the audition found that the band played Calypso Island style music!

2. When replying to ads <u>be courteous</u> and professional. I firmly believe in making a strong first impression. Remember, if you don't hack it in your initial contact, it could be your last.

3. <u>Don't lie</u> about anything. Not your age, experience, gear... whatever. Lies tend to catch up with you sooner or later and only complicate matters. And if you do happen to get the job, you'll have to live the lie.

4. Make sure you're <u>clear</u> on all interview or audition details, and if in doubt – ask!

5. Before the audition (if possible), try and see the band or buy their album and <u>familiarize</u> yourself with their music.

6. Get a good night's <u>sleep</u> to ensure that you are at your freshest and most alert when you audition.

7. <u>No substances</u>. Don't use anything to increase your chances, rather keep a natural clear head. As Dom Famularo once told me, "I've never heard of a successful drug story". Too true!

8. <u>Don't be late</u>! Arrive in good time so that you aren't flustered.

9. Remember that everyone is bound to be nervous, whether a little or a lot. Put your doubt and fears to the back of your mind by putting in the necessary groundwork and <u>believe</u> that you can do it. If you find you are nervous then try breathing deeply and slowly as this will help you relax.

10. <u>Don't concern yourself</u> with the other drummers at the audition. You're all there for the same reason so don't let anyone intimidate you.

11. If you have managed to listen to the band's material and prepared yourself, then play what you've heard and don't experiment. If the band wants something different they'll ask you. If you've never heard any of the material then play straight and don't be too clever or fancy as you'll open yourself up to making mistakes. Most importantly, <u>listen carefully</u> to what is happening around you and just do the best you can.

12. When the audition is over, <u>thank everyone and leave</u>. Don't hang around and ask questions like, "hey, how did I do?" or "was I okay?" If you've taken care of business and fit the band's image, they'll call you and tell you so.

13. If the band says they'll call you to tell you whether you're onto the next level, <u>don't be a pest</u> and bug them with persistent phone calls as this could switch them right off. If they don't call you after a reasonable period of time then assume you didn't get the job – I know it can be tough but that's the way it is. However, if you're really keen and convinced you got the job, then make a short courteous call to check the position. I once did this after what I thought was a very good audition. I hadn't heard anything and decided to give the band a call – just to make sure that I had not got the job. Turned out to be a good call as I found out that they'd been frantically trying to get hold of me but couldn't because they'd misplaced my contact details. So we were all pleased I made the call. In a situation like this my advice is use your own judgment and common sense.

14. If you don't get the job then forget about it and <u>move on</u>. Don't dwell on why you didn't get it. Most of the time you won't find out the reason anyway, so just accept the decision and

keep on looking. With enough perseverance, the right attitude and being honest with yourself, you'll find what you're looking for.

15. When presenting material whether audio or visual, ensure that the instant the START button is pressed that you grab the listeners or viewers attention. In all auditions, especially major ones, (remember my interview?!) make the best use of your time because time is always extremely limited in these situations.

16. If you're asked to comment on the leaving band member then don't criticize. Be tactful and show respect for their work.

to sum up

Finally, the factor I consider all-important and above everything else is to **ALWAYS BE YOURSELF**. You only really ever get into trouble when you try to be someone or something you're not. If you practice smart, do your homework, take care of business, listen to what's going on around you and relax, the situation will more often than not take care of itself.

So take the sting out of auditioning by using from this chapter what you need to implement into your personal situation and increase your audition success rate.

Don't Quit
'When things go wrong, as they sometimes will,
When the road you're trudging seems all up hill,
When the funds are low and the debts are high,
All you want to do is sigh,
When care is pressing you down a bit,
Rest, if you must – but don't you quit.

Success is failure turned inside out,
The silver tint of the clouds of doubt,
And you never can tell how close you are,
It may be near when it seems afar,
So stick to the fight when you're hardest hit
It's when things seem worst that you must not quit'

– Unknown Author

working with established names and celebrities

My first experience of working with a celebrity came as a 16 year old when I played my first residency in a Greek restaurant.

We (the band) were hired to provide the music for a body-building contest (of all things) to take place in our local Town Hall. The evening's proceedings were as follows: We were to open the show with a song of our choice and thereafter, provide the backing music for the contestants while they strutted their stuff on stage. The first half of the show would then close with the band playing another tune. After intermission the MC, who was a nationally renowned radio and TV personality, would open the second half of the show with a short cabaret spot. This would comprise two tunes where the band would be required to provide the backing. The contestants would then come back on for the final judging, with us once again providing the backing music. Finally, the show would come to an end with us playing the final tune – simple!

here's how it went

On the day of the show we transported our gear to the venue in the early afternoon. We'd been informed that a rehearsal would take place for our benefit. The rehearsal comprised the organizer telling us what type of music was required and giving us an idea of how long each event would run. By not being present, the celebrity MC would inform us of his requirements before the show. So not much of a rehearsal really!

Anyway, evening came and I headed over to the venue.

All my school buddies knew about the event and I had also told everyone else I knew that I would be playing at the show. So, while standing in the wings I spotted many of my friends in the audience. I was looking forward to getting up on stage as most of them had never seen me play before and I was eager to show them what I could do.

Eventually the curtains opened and we launched into our opening song. It finished to generous applause and then the show got under way. The first half went smoothly with no problems. So far so good – smiles all round.

During the interval our celebrity MC came over to discuss his cabaret spot. He was an accomplished pianist and it transpired that the only member of the band he required to back him was ME on drums! Briefly he explained the format of the two songs and then we were ready to go.

Once again the curtains opened and we launched into the second half of the show with a swing tune. The celebrity sang and played... and I did my thing. Every now and then he'd look at me with a smiling but oddly pained expression on his face. "Hey", I thought in my boundless youthful enthusiasm, "what a great guy, he must really like me – I'm doing great"! So I smiled squarely back at him. The first tune ended and our MC thanked the audience for the appreciative applause. He engaged in a little patter and then launched us into a quick 2/4 show tune. I was fairly familiar with the general arrangement so it didn't present a problem. "Good on you Georg" I thought, "you're doing great"!

As quickly as it began, the short cabaret spot ended to a round of generous applause and the rest of the show continued... and closed, without a hitch. Whew, my first big show and a job well done....?

FREE Well-meaning advice

While we were packing up our gear, the celebrity came over, shook my hand and thanked me for backing him. He then proceeded to offer me a piece of friendly advice. He told me I had been way too loud and that in future if I ever back cabaret again, to be more sympathetic to the featured artist by not drowning them out with excess volume.

I met him again much later on in life and on reflection, can state that he really was and is a great guy, and meant well in offering me his wise and experienced <u>free</u> advice. But I, being 16 and totally invincible took it all with a pinch of salt and decided that he was an *oldie* and out of touch with modern drumming – he didn't know what he was taking about. Well, he <u>did know</u> what he was talking about... as I was to learn over the coming years.

the hired hand

Some artists give you little or no freedom to play outside of what they want to hear, whereas others allow you the freedom to be more creative. However, the bottom line of this chapter is to realize that whenever you work with a big name or any artist regardless of stature, you're there to make <u>them</u> sound (and look) good. Yup, you're the hired hand, not the main attraction. Your job is to play what <u>they</u> want to hear, not what you <u>want</u> them to hear. So if you're too much of an individualist and find it hard to compromise on what you like to play, then perhaps this line of work won't suit. You may find resentment building up due to the creative limitations imposed and be without a job before too long. The reality of this scenario is that the audience has bought tickets to see the artist – not you. Sure, you may be an integral part of the backing band, but once again remember you're there to provide a service. When you get this into perspective and wear the right attitude, this kind of gig becomes a whole lot easier and pleasant to handle.

Personally, in having backed various artists in many different situations, I now try to restrict myself to those gigs that I know I'll enjoy and which will allow me to express my musical ideas.

both sides of the coin

One big name I worked with was great when the show was going well, but heaven help the band if something wasn't quite right – whether it was us at fault or not! No, if anything went wrong then it would always the band at fault. No way did he ever entertain the idea for one second that perhaps it could have been <u>him</u>. On the other hand, if the audience wasn't very responsive he'd spend virtually half the show with his back to them, drawing support from us (his backing band) and not once did he give us credit for being his *crutch*.

Once while on tour, I overheard this dude imparting advice to the (younger) singer of the support act for our show. He said that all musicians were expendable and could be replaced at the drop of a hat. Great advice huh? Okay, granted, it is true that there will always be someone waiting in the wings to replace you. But when you're out there busting your chops night after night, it's nice to get some credit from the artist you're working hard to make look and sound good. Perhaps I should have told him one night before going on stage that I refused to play and was leaving the band, and see how quickly he dropped *his* hat? Nah, I was too much of a pro to do that and had more self respect. Today, I'm a lot older and a lot wiser and wouldn't back anyone who didn't show me equal respect. But as I always say; there is another side to the coin.

I have had great pleasure in working with top artists who treated the band as part of their act and not merely the faceless backing band. One such situation was with a UK female vocalist who has done countless TV and radio appearances, and is extremely well respected as she has an outstanding voice. She always thanks her musicians and always has time for a friendly chat regardless of her star status. Nice lady!

These two pretty extreme scenarios are given purely to illustrate that they do occur. But different as they are, there is a thread that runs through and connects them. In both cases I was expected to play exactly what each artist wanted to hear and nothing else. But you sure operate better when you work with someone who appreciates you.

Big names can be anyone from TV hosts, comedians, illusionists, instrumentalists, singers, etc. And one of the biggest advantages of these types of gigs is that they are usually well paid. So it stands to reason that in this line of work it's never a good idea to take up an argument with the bandleader or musical director to *heated* levels as you may well lose your job, even if you know you're right – in a case like this, swallow that bitter pill. Buddy Rich got away with this, but then again that was Buddy Rich!

good time and good feel

For most stars, the most important ingredient they require from you (the drummer) is to keep good time. And good time may not even necessarily mean metronomic time, but following and playing to the singer's time and phrasing. Mark Shulman who has worked with many big names says that when backing Cher, he takes his cue for tempo from her body movement. I read an article a while back on how one of Ray Charles' drummers would take his cue for time and tempo from Ray's stomping foot.

In a more general sense, a singer who also plays an instrument, such as an acoustic guitar, may require you to listen closely and play to the time being laid down by their strumming. In addition to the timing they'll also want you to play with the correct feel to their style of music. These *time and feel* qualities are paramount and take preference over anything else. A real life example of this is from a drummer I know who backed folk singer Janis Ian and said he took his cue for time from her acoustic guitar.

to sum up

Yes! Stars can at times be temperamental and in my experience I've found singers to generally have the least patience. I do understand this because, after all, it's their reputations on the line whenever they step out on stage with nothing but a microphone between them and the audience. I suppose if I were the featured star and had to battle through a show while one of the band was trashing things behind me, I'd have strong words to say about it – especially since it would be me signing his or her pay check. I'd have assumed they'd taken on the gig because they had wanted it and knew what was required, and had the ability to handle it. Right? But we're not just talking drummer here, we're talking guitarist, backing vocals, bass, keyboard... whatever.

Quite simply: play what the man (or lady) wants and everybody will be happy – including you.

how to achieve your best onstage drum mix

As a drummer one of the most frustrating things for me has always been trying to project the 'sound' I have in my head to the audience. What I mean by this is that I am pretty envious of guitarists or keyboard players who have an array of effects pedals or processors on hand to do this, and where this sound is projected back at them from their immediate monitoring system or amp – as this is 'their' sound which they have created. I found this especially evident in my earlier drumming days when playing in cover material bands, whereby I may have needed to play a track that had a huge reverb drum sound on the original studio recording and felt disappointed in the sound coming back at me from my unprocessed acoustic drum kit. Sure, the sound may have been processed in the front of house PA, but from MY immediate perspective I would be hearing this 'small' unprocessed sound – not that there's anything wrong with a well tuned acoustic kit, it's just that to me this has always one the frustrating things about acoustic drums.

Okay, since those early days (and for me this means the late 70's and early 80's) technology has advanced greatly. But you may be wondering why I never asked for reverb in my monitors to 'fatten' my immediate sound perspective. Well firstly, drum monitors were a relative luxury in those days and secondly as I started to play bigger and better gigs with monitoring, I found that I preferred to have an untreated drum (and music) mix in my onstage monitors as this made me play tighter – especially in halls or theatres which had a lot of natural reverb. The last thing I wanted was my 'immediate' processed reverb competing with the natural acoustics of the venue. Those musicians who have played venues with a high roof and where you get a vicious slap back off the back wall will know what I'm talking about. Incidentally, I have the same approach when recording in that I don't want any effects (especially delay) in my cans as this often makes the mix muddy and harder to lock into and find the pocket. But saying that, do bear in mind that what might be a nightmare for one person may be a dream for another. However, despite this, achieving an inspiring and balanced onstage mix is I believe, one of the most challenging areas in audio reproduction as there are usually so many variables involved – unlike the studio environment which is much easier to control.

Let's face it, if you have a bad onstage sound then this can be very uninspiring and even ruin a potentially great gig. A good example may be where you're in a band which has its own rig and plays a show one night where everything sounds amazing and you really get your rocks off - then the next night in a different venue with the exact same gear the onstage sound sucks and is totally abysmal. Gremlins in the mix? Read on...

the path to stress-free onstage drum mixes

Before I carry on I need to point out that I am not here to offer any specific information on mixing techniques or technical advice. No, this is such a vast area of expertise in itself and very subjective, as a drum mix is personal to each and every drummer and depends on the genre of music. If you want more info of this then check out specialist work books that deal specifically with this area of music. And it's worth doing as I believe the more we know about the technicalities of our respective instruments and related areas, then the better this is for us. Knowledge = power.

Okay, so what kind of solutions can drummers (and indeed other musicians) employ to achieve a more satisfying and consistent onstage sound or mix? Well firstly, I'm going to go back to the subject of getting an onstage sound that inspires you and which gives you what YOU expect to hear.

If you're playing music where the drum sound doesn't need to vary too much sonically, then you simply need to get the best mix of 'your' immediately pleasing acoustic drum sound – in other words, that which sounds good to YOU. And how you achieve this is down to your immediate situation. Do you have a permanent 'front of house' (FOH) engineer who also controls the onstage sound, or if your band is really happening do you have a separate monitor mix engineer? Or is it really down to basics in where it's just you and not a monitor in sight? Yep, I've been there and got all those T-shirts!

If it's the former then you need to relay exactly what you require in your drum mix, and then from the full band mix. Do you need more bass guitar in order to better lock in, or do you want to hear a more balanced mix as if listening to a studio recording. Whatever you settle on, make sure that these settings are stored whether digitally or otherwise so that they are called up on every gig and you always get the same sound, no matter what the surrounding acoustics are. And how do you ensure that the venues acoustics won't ruin your perfect personal mix? IN-EAR MONITORING – that how! What you have in your mix is a personal choice, but a set of pro quality in-ear monitors will solve almost any acoustical nightmare whether it's a bad room or an unsympathetic engineer. Your own consistent personal mix will always give you as much control of your immediate personal space as you can achieve. If you have the peace of mind in knowing that you have a permanent engineer who will always give you what you want in your mix then cool, you're sorted out. But if you are having to rely on a different FOH and/or monitor engineer every show, then the easiest way to a stress free existence is to do it yourself. Achieve this by using your own mixer onstage and control your own mix! You may not be able to control what it sounds like out front, but if your onstage sound is happening then you're gonna play a whole lot better and enjoy every gig. This to me is the ultimate goal.

Now if it was the latter scenario where you don't have an engineer and are in a band where it's just you and your trusty acoustic kit with no drum mics (and the rest of the band is drowning you out due to excessive volume), then you need to resolve this tricky situation one way or another. Firstly, I hope you're wearing some form of hearing protectors. Secondly if the band refuses to turn down even after you've shown them your bleeding hands (and ears) and you still really believe in this outfit, then you need to find a way to project your sound more efficiently, or at least hear yourself better. So what solutions?

A set of (cheap?) drum mics would be the first option for me... that is if the bands PA system can handle the low end frequencies of the kick drum? Or what about triggering electronic sounds to beef up the acoustic kit level? Bear in mind that these are merely starting points and as every situation is unique, you need to resolve your personal situation in a manner which works for everyone: whatever the end result? However and additionally, the option of considering an in-ear monitor option here as well should be taken very seriously, because not only do they give you a clear mix directly into your ears, they also cut out excessive outside volume and therefore double as ear defenders. Sounds like a win-win situation to me!

I've mainly discussed up to now the requirements for a drum sound which maybe doesn't need to vary too much in timbre. But what about playing music where you may need to provide more than one drum set mix/sound? Maybe you need different snare drum sounds, tight high pitched toms and also thunderous deep tom sounds, a compressed tight kick sound but also a rounder jazzier sound with resonance? The answer lies in electronics, unless you prefer to have a huge setup from hell and an articulated truck to move your gear. If you're okay moving over to the dark side and playing a complete electronic setup then this is a great option. This solution offers a virtually endless array of drum sounds and will also certainly make the engineer very happy as there will be no onstage drum mics to encourage feedback. But if the idea of an electronic setup leaves you cold and you still want to play acoustic drums (I know I do), then triggering drum sounds via pads or triggers through a suitable module (brain) will give you the sound variations you require.

to sum up

As drummers and specifically acoustic kit drummers, the challenge of recording and re-enforcing the sound of our instruments electronically can often prove to be difficult. In my opinion the more control we can have over our sound in a live situation, the better the end result. There are of course limits to what we can do and achieve, as the sound we want to hear and may achieve onstage, may not always be faithfully reproduced to the audience. This is an aspect of live sound which most of the time we have no control over and should learn to accept. But if we can be master of the immediate sound and mix that we hear, then this will ensure that we at least have more good gigs than bad ones. And then if all comes together in where the people responsible for the sound out front reproduce what we'd like the audience to hear, then this to me is the ultimate goal in live sound.

In retrospect, of all the live (and studio) work that I have done, most of the time everybody has been on the same page and focused on achieving the best result, which is a great sound. So be agreeable and cool with everyone concerned when it comes to sound, as the people responsible wield a lot of power over the end result. And if you do experience the odd occasion where you work with somebody who is difficult or maybe not switched on, then be diplomatic and do the best you can. There's always the next gig...

how to be creative in any musical situation

The Oxford English Dictionary defines creativity as 'bringing into being' or 'giving rise to'. *Bringing into being* is the definition I like because when I'm drawing on my creative sources I feel as though I am bringing into being that musical knowledge which is stored in my *personal library* of musical information. Actually, *giving rise* to is a pretty similar definition because you're allowing your creative abilities to rise to the surface.

Lets get specific

In the previous chapter, in dealing with stars, I discussed how musically restricting a situation like this can sometimes be. So, to make any repetitive gig interesting, you have to find ways of being as musically creative as you can possibly be, within the framework laid down by the artist you're working for. It's the same when working in a restrictive situation such as playing to diners in a restaurant – you have to play what's appropriate for the venue and musical requirements. In any situation like this you have to dig deep into your creativity to ensure you don't get bored, while still doing a good job in delivering what's required.

For example: I remember back to my first pro gig in a high class cabaret restaurant which I played for over a year – five nights a week. The first set would consist of background music played at an extremely low volume level so that the diners could easily converse. In this set we played standards, swing tunes, ballads, Latin tunes, and so on. This set provided a challenge in that I needed to play with intensity at a low volume level.

This improved my control and also gave me the opportunity to experiment using not only sticks but also brushes. In the Latin tunes I would sometimes disengage the snare mechanism and play with my bare hands to try gain a more authentic sound and feel. I also used mallets, timbale sticks and multi-rods for further timbres and colors. In short, I applied many variables to make my drumming sound good and make that quiet first set, fun and interesting, within the framework required. The second set was a gear up and featured a few more up-tempo numbers encouraging the diners to dance, but while still having to keep the volume low for the remaining diners. My creativity now shifted to a different area in establishing a good solid groove and feel in the dance numbers. My objective here was to supply that groove that was punchy and intense, but at that lower volume level. Once again, a great control exercise

Then came the cabaret spot – and this could be any kind of situation. Sometimes a singer, or a magician, even a comedian where the band wasn't required at all for backing up the artist. But when we did have back up the artist then the challenges here would always be very different. Sometimes we'd have a rehearsal but most times not. We might get good charts, sometimes very sketchy charts, and a lot of the time have to sight-read them. The cabaret spot was normally the *wake up* and play on *edge of your seat* section, as anything could and usually did happen.

After the cabaret, we played our last set which usually featured out and out dancing material where the volume allowed me to stretch out and play harder. Now my creativity was tested in a different direction by the quality and variation of the pop, disco, rock beats and fills required without straying too far from the confines of the music. Then of course having to shift gears by dropping the volume and tempo for the last of the *smooch* songs of the evening.

So as you see, this was a varied gig with a lot of different aspects and applications to it. Sure, like anything else it could have become boring as some aspects of the gig were repetitive and I could have resorted to merely going through the motions in order to get through the night. Instead, I enjoyed the challenge of making the gig interesting and as varied as I could. I also enjoyed the free meals and generous salary. You call this working...?

You may ask, "is creativity allied to being versatile"? I think it is and applies whether you've chosen to become an all-rounder by being accomplished in various styles, or choosing to be accomplished within one style of music. Let me explain...

While working with an award winning country band (my main gig), I also gigged with another band whose style of music was funkier, with a rock edge. This band allowed me to stretch out and play far busier and complex drumming, whereas my drumming in the country-oriented band was more restricted, requiring me to play straighter and simpler.

One night, the leader of the country band came to a gig I was doing with the other outfit. After the first set he said to me, "you must find what we do really boring because you have to play very straight". My answer was, "yes, I do play straight and simpler, but bored I'm not"! By this I meant that my approach was to play the set rhythms as well as I could – every time – and always strive to make the music groove as much as possible by giving it the best feel I could. When there were short drum breaks offering the opportunity to improvise, then I'd draw on my creative sources to come up with something just that little bit different, adding a sparkle to the song yet still staying within the boundaries of that style of music.

I personally believe that creative improvisation stems from two sources. The first is a natural ability inherent in the individual to come up with ideas to express themselves. The second source is a learned one... developed from a lot of research, a lot of practice and extensive performance experience. The result of the latter source is a huge bank of creative information (tools) stored in the mind to draw upon, while the natural inherent ability serves as a vehicle to deliver this information, which results in creative improvisation.

I've reached the point where for much of the time, my playing occurs on a sub-conscious level. This means I'm not consciously thinking about everything I play, but allowing my sub-conscious to draw on that vast library of information which is the beats, fills, polyrhythmic figures, linear patterns, rudimental studies, my concept of feel, my approach to time – in fact everything I've ever practiced and performed over the years. I believe that regardless of how much natural ability a person may possess, without having this bank of stored information gained from extensive practice and performance, I can't see how they can creatively improvise, because these two elements have to co-exist to be able to play what is required on a creative level.

Whenever I write my own material, I do this on keyboard. Not being the most competent of players, my keyboard knowledge and playing ability is fairly limited, however I am presently taking lessons to improve my skill and knowledge. Therefore, I only have a small bank of technical keyboard creativity (information) to draw on. So how do I get round this stumbling block? Well, from listening to many forms of music over the years, I utilize that vast bank of *general* musical knowledge to help me create. For example, I have the ability to create a jazz solo vocally, but don't ask me to play it on a keyboard because I couldn't. So when I find I'm stuck for ideas due to my lack of technical ability, I sing into a microphone and record new ideas that (normally) wouldn't surface due to my limited keyboard skills. From there, because the sung part has been recorded, I'll eventually work it out on keys. Another thing to add here is that because I have limited keyboard skills, there is a tendency for whatever I write to sound too much the same. And this will also apply to a drummer with limited stored information, in that they will only produce what their limitations allow them to play.

So I believe that limited knowledge = limited creativity.

to sum up

I advocate that to be musically creative, drummers need to devote a lot of time to research and practice of their instrument. Research being in the form of playing, listening to other drummers, experimenting within music styles and everything else connected with the drums. Constant practice then reinforces all this research and builds up a personal creative bank of knowledge.

All this knowledge is not only great when you're pushing the limits of your creativity by engaging in the highest levels of playing, but it also helps when you're playing simpler forms of music. Also, this stored knowledge doesn't necessarily have to be endowed with technical prowess either. Look around and see how many drummers earning huge pay packets are not technical wizards, but great feel-merchants. They have arrived at this point by extensive rehearsing and performance, achieving a masterly, creative command of their instrument, whether in jazz, rock, fusion, country or any multitude of styles.

the overplaying factor

Virtually every drummer on this planet will admit to going through a period of *overplaying* (playing in excess of what the music requires) – usually in the formative years of their career.

When I started playing in the early 70's my musical influences were bands like 'Emerson Lake and Palmer' (ELP), 'Yes', 'Jethro Tull', 'Kansas', etc – as you can see all in the progressive rock genre. Now, those of you familiar with these bands of that era will remember most of the music they played was extremely complex at the best of times. I especially remember when Billy Cobham broke onto the scene with 'The Mahavishnu Orchestra'. *Cobham-itis* seemed to afflict virtually every drummer I knew, as they were all trying to implement his style of drumming into their own. I too, when young, eager and musically immature, would strive to impress by incorporating this style of drumming into whatever I played – whether it suited the music or not. Trying to copy those busy patterns Carl Palmer laid down was great for developing my technique, but created a nightmare for the other musicians I worked with. I'm not knocking technique here as I love the more complex side of drumming, however, there is an appropriate time and place for everything. In those early days my lines of thought would usually be something like, "hey ...this'll impress 'em, I'll stick this (unnecessary) fast fill in here" or, "look drummers here it comes, wadabadabada (totally out of context drum part) all the time thinking "aren't I good"?...

Well, I certainly made people aware of my technique skills and how fast I could play, but at the same time developed a

reputation for being a far-too-busy drummer. Funnily enough, I didn't mind this label and was proud of my *technical* reputation. In retrospect, this label would have fitted better had it been tagged more appropriately. The reason why I overplayed so much was that I rarely got the chance to play the music I was so influenced by. As a result, whenever I did play, I'd try to incorporate this busy drumming style into any music I played, however simple or complex. Some liked it, most didn't. Fortunately, at the time I wasn't relying on music for a living, so pretty much played what and with whom I wanted. I did eventually join a rock band playing complex material and got the chance to get rid of a lot of this pent up musical frustration.

One size shoe does not fit all

As time passed and with more experience gained, I woke up to the fact that one style of drumming didn't suit all types of music. So, if I was going to survive as a professional musician, I'd have to change my attitude.

My biggest attitude shift came when I started working with a good friend. Guiseppe (Peps for short) is a complete musician in that aside from being an accomplished keyboard player and vocalist he also has one of the best sets of ears in the business. By this I mean when listening to music whether for pleasure or work, he listens to everything, and not just his keyboard related parts. In particular, I remember back to us sitting in his folks' lounge one evening listening to a Gino Vannelli album. The track was *Brother to Brother* with the incredible Mark Craney on drums. While we listened, Peps started pointing out things to me that I wasn't hearing. Factors like the overall production; how the phrasing of the voice worked with the underlying rhythms; zoning in on each instrument individually – in short listening to the whole song and not just the drums. You may be thinking that this all sounds too common sense-like, after all when you listen to music, well ... you just listen! Wrong! It's amazing how many drummers listen with only half an ear. The fact is that as instrumentalists it's so easy for us to get wrapped up in only our instrument and ignore what's happening musically around us. This makes for an unmusical drummer.

If you're not listening to the music in the first place, then when you sit down to play you won't be playing the music, but only playing the drums. This may sound like a riddle, but I remember reading an article in which Steve Gadd expressed this beautifully by saying that when he plays, he doesn't play the drums, but plays the song.

In light of all I've said so far, I'm now going to make a contradictory statement: I don't regard overplaying as too much of a bad thing, because I feel this to be a natural progression for young players to pass through in order to become more musical drummers. However, in the same breath... I am not here endorsing overplaying! The reality is that the majority of developing young drummers will do this anyway. And I strongly believe that in order for anyone to develop into a well-rounded drummer, the technical side has to be explored. It's a bit like a kid trying all the candy in a store and then settling on preferred flavors.

The other reality is that when you try and restrict someone from doing what they want to do, what happens? They rebel! So for drummers, it's a far better thing to thrash away and get this 'wanting-to-play-everything' factor out of the system. Then with time and experience, this *overplaying* element literally *plays itself out* and they start settling down to play more appropriately and tastefully.

ways of coping

Should you find yourself in the position where you're being criticized by others for overplaying, then there are solutions to this situation. The most obvious would be to leave the band or show. But if you're enjoying the music, then try finding an outlet, such as a suitable part-time band where you can thrash away to your heart's content, or if possible play to appropriate recorded music at home. In other words, get your rocks off and get rid of the frustration. I'm a good example: When I played with the country band the drumming was pretty restrictive. So outside of that band I took on jazz gigs allowing me to stretch out. Also, when time allowed, I wrote and recorded material incorporating my own preferred drumming style.

I do appreciate that my example can't suit everyone, but there are always alternatives. As mentioned earlier, the easiest solution is to play along to music that you enjoy. However, this could become sterile after a while because of the lack of interaction with other musicians. So how about seeking out a jam session night in your area? These are usually a lot of fun. If there isn't one, maybe you can start your own? Another avenue might be to put your own *jam* band together by advertising for like-minded musicians who like yourself, may be looking for some form of frustration buster. And if you can't jam at home then perhaps a rehearsal studio might be the best solution for everybody?

These are merely suggestions and if you really are serious about doing something like this, then put your thinking cap on and get something going. The object is to have fun and play what you want to play.

to sum up

We all have different opinions on how and what we should play, so overplaying can at times be a judgment call. You might not always agree with others regarding overplaying criticism and I don't think there's anything wrong with that. So don't just blindly accept what other people say. However, I say this only as far as you being totally honest with yourself and also being open to constructive opinion. If still in doubt, then the quickest way to clear this up is to record yourself. Then, depending on what style of music you're playing, you can check out how adventurous and complimentary (or not) you're being to the music. If it's cover material then your reference will be the original recorded track. If it's in an original music band situation then listen to recordings of similar examples of the music you're playing and make honest comparisons.

Finally, remember this: always keep an open mind to different ideas and theories to improve your standard of drumming.

demo packages – making them work for you

For us instrumentalists, I believe that putting together a demo package (DP) is only of any use when we're responding directly to a 'drummer wanted' ad, or if somebody directly requests one from us. This is because in the past I've spent a lot of time and money sending off DP's to recording studios or management companies, in the feint hope of securing session and/or live work. I personally have only ever secured session work when someone from a studio has seen or heard me play, or when I've been personally recommended. Let's face it, studio time is very expensive and no producer is going to take a chance on someone they don't know. They'd rather use a tried-and-tested drummer, or a drummer that the tried-and-tested drummer recommends.

While living in northern England I was *house* drummer for a recording studio. This meant that I did all their drum sessions. The engineer booked me because he knew he could count on me coming up with what he required and was very reluctant to use anyone else. And whenever he did use somebody else, it was on my recommendation.

"Okay", you might be saying, "this makes perfect sense, but it leaves me in a catch-22 situation because if I don't know any industry people, then how am I going to get a personal recommendation"? (*See chapter 12*). Well, my answer to that is that you need to let people know who you are by getting out there and putting yourself on *show*. This means you need to play as much as you can, meet the people that count and build up contacts – in other words, <u>network</u>. Additionally, your personal

DP plays an important role in helping you achieve this.

Although a DP may not always work if you are trying to break into studio work, when it comes to any other areas like answering 'drummer wanted' ads, I honestly believe it's vital to have the best looking DP that you can summon up. You see... your DP is *your* personal recommendation, and the better the recommendation, the more chance you have of getting the gig you want. Then the more you play, the more you're seen and so the process of breaking out of the catch-22 situation begins. This is exactly how I did it many years ago. Many times I would play gigs for little or no money, but the payback was that I spread the word of who I was and what I could do – and so began the process of personal recommendations. Ask any well-known drummer how they got to where they are today and they will tell you a similar story.

What a good demo package contains

The first thing to consider is that the content of your DP will depend on what area of music you're involved in and also what the specific (job) angle is.

For major auditions original bands often request DP's as they want to make sure that your image and influences match theirs. By reviewing the packages first they save themselves a lot of time and reduce the need to see hordes of applicants, then from the strength of these packages they can make up a short list of the people they wish to see.

A cover band might also request a package, especially if they have a strong image and definitive sound. For example, they may be a revivalist group playing only Beatles songs and be really dedicated in putting forward a strong image and that *original* Beatles sound. A cover band playing functions such as weddings and Bar Mitzvahs may have no definitive image or sound, and might be more flexible and focus on just your drumming and/or reading skills (and vocal ability if required).

Before proceeding further it needs to be mentioned that this new edition of 'Rhythm of the Head' has updated information on how to effectively market yourself on the internet. This is presented in greater detail in Chapter 25. Whether you choose the more traditional option of sending out your information via ordinary mail, or take the internet option with email, the advice offered applies to both methods of delivery. The mode of delivery (the how) is not the issue focus here, it is what you include and present in your DP that is the primary focus in this chapter.

In the past I've employed various methods in putting together effective DP's and I wholeheartedly recommend that you try some or even all of what I suggest... that is, if you haven't already discovered these for yourself. Here goes:

the content

The photograph. The image represented in your photograph should reflect the style of music you're into and be a recent shot. If you're in a position to employ the services of a professional photographer, then I strongly advise you do so. If you can't afford this service but have a good quality digital camera or have a friend with one, then ask them to take some shots. With a little perseverance and imagination you should end up with some good usable pictures.

Give thought to the content of the photos. Do you want a live action shot behind your drums, or a static standing shot in either a studio or outside location? Do you feel comfortable posing or would you rather present a more relaxed image by being photographed while walking? Do you want to make a feature of your gear? You may have a large impressive looking drum setup and feel it relevant to show this off in the hope that it increases your chances of getting an audition or job.

Whether you choose to utilize the services of a pro photographer or not, your aim should be to produce the best looking photos you can manage, whatever your budget and image.

The biography. This should contain all the key points required in the most concise form. My biographies have at times contained all or only some of the following. Choose the points that apply to you:

a) name – if you have a stage name, state it;
b) contact address and telephone numbers;
c) age – if required;
d) a brief description of your equipment;
e) your transport availability;
f) your commitments (if any) and availability;
g) a short summary of your musical influences and favorite drummers;
h) a brief description of your live work history – bands you've played with, theatre work, important shows, sessions etc;
i) list any achievements – grade examinations attained in

music, degrees, certificates, courses etc;

 j) give information on any recording experience with bands or sessions. Describe the processes of recording – working with click tracks, no clicks, overdubbing tom fills, overdubbing snare, programming etc;

 k) give a brief description of your musical aspirations, where you'd like to see yourself, your ideal band situation and so on.

The demo CD or DVD. Here again, be as professional as you can get. Never use cheap quality disks. If your potential band members or the producer is trying to listen to a disk that is skipping or doesn't even load properly, then it's going to land up in only one place – the trash can.

Make sure your recording is as good as you can get. If you're recording yourself at a live gig, then attempt to get the cleanest sound you can manage. If you're only showcasing your drumming (without music) and don't have the means of recording at home, then booking into a budget recording studio to achieve this may be the option – the initial expense could be well worth it in the long run. The same applies to any DVD footage – make sure it looks and sounds good. If in doubt, then ask other (knowledgeable) people to assess this for you and proceed from their comments.

Your demo should contain no more than three full songs (or see below for an alternative). Pick the best examples of your playing and if you're showcasing a drum solo, then make sure it grabs the listener's attention from the first note. Pack all you can into around two minutes (or less), ensuring that what is being showcased is relevant to the situation you're applying for. Again, for constructive criticism and feedback you may want to play your solo to other musicians for their opinion to help you settle on your chosen solo section. If you impress them, then you'll impress others.

you may want to try this

To get more variety and examples onto your DP, record short excerpts of your playing. Make these around 30 seconds to one minute in length. By doing this you can now do one of two things: You can present one long continuous track in which there will be no breaks between these excerpts. The aim here is to encourage *unbroken* attentive listening to the continuous flow of music. So what you end up with is one anything from three to six minutes long, with five to six examples of your playing as opposed to three separate tracks lasting say twelve minutes, which is twice as long. If you choose this method and one of the excerpts starts at the beginning of a song, then make that one the first to start off your demo. If all the excerpts are sections within songs, then start the first excerpt off with a pro fade in, and then fade this out into the next track, doing the same for the rest of the tracks.

The second option is to still present short excerpts, but to have breaks between each one. With this method you give the listener the opportunity to zone in on a track of their choice, or to skip between tracks if they so wish. Whether you use the first method or second, this is a judgment call and will depend on what kind of gig you're applying for. However, irrespective of which method you choose, you'll find you can cram more onto your demo and present the strongest representations of your playing by *cutting to the chase*. What this means is you should only choose parts in songs that best represent your playing. For example, you may have played a killer fill towards the end of a song, which more than likely will be missed should the listener only listen to the first few seconds of that particular track. So cue that track from the killer fill and grab the listener's attention right away. Makes sense doesn't it?

Aside from the above, you should present a track listing in the order of play. In my listings I have at times included some or all of the following information. Once again, decide what works best for you,

Track style. Rock ballad, dance track, R&B soul, big band tune etc. I personally don't tend to offer song titles because it's my drumming I'm showcasing, not the song. However, there have been times when I've given a song title if it's been presented for an award or has charted. Why? Always use whatever ammo you have to impress people – don't be shy – you've worked for it and deserve it!

Method of recording. Briefly describe how you've played the drum parts. For example: played an acoustic kit with click track; sequenced kick and snare drum with tom overdubs; live acoustic set with no click; all drums programmed with live percussion overdubs, and so on. If you're hunting down session work then feature various recording methods to show how versatile you can be in the studio.

Duration of tracks. As mentioned above, you can have

one longer continuous track, or punchy excerpts with breaks inbetween each one. Which ever, give your listener the information they need so they know what they're listening to and the duration of the main track or tracks.

Demo cover and label. Once again there are two options open to you. The first is to utilize the services of a printing company that specializes in putting together covers for CDs and DVDs. If you can afford this option then by all means use it, as you will (or should) land up with a great looking product. However, most musicians especially when starting out don't have this kind of budget, and are forced to take the DIY route. I've put together some pretty good covers on a shoestring budget – here's how.

Should you want to use a photo on the cover then consider using a black and white shot. This can look very affective and is much cheaper and easier to photocopy. Color copying might look cool but can be pretty expensive with the cost mounting up when producing quite a few demos.

Once you have your chosen photo you'll need to re-size this to fit a standard CD or DVD case. For the inner sleeve there are a number of options open to you. My suggestion is to check out some of your favorite CD's (or DVD's) and get ideas for presentation. Then produce the artwork on an appropriate design program. If you're unable to do this yourself but maybe have a friend who can, then ask them. If none of this works for you, then you may have to resort to the pricier option of hiring someone to do this for you. If this doesn't work either, then check out your local college or university Arts department. Many times you can hook up with students who will be very keen to become involved with bands or musicians. I remember back to when I was playing in a very *arty* band. We were a happening young band and had many arts students falling over themselves to design for us – and they didn't want money for this either – just the credit and enough to cover expenses. This is because it's a cool thing for them to do and a creative outlet for what they're studying.

The cover letter. Yes, you need a covering letter and whether you choose a business-like or less formal approach, this should always look and sound professional. With personal computer technology today it is relatively cheap to design your own professional looking letterhead. More than likely you will only require a few letterheads at a time, so print these out when required and keep your costs down. Once again, if you can't do this yourself then ask a friend.

The content of your covering letter should be no more than just an introduction. If you're answering a *drummer wanted* ad then refer to this and mention any person you may have spoken to in your initial response and address the letter to whoever is handling the auditions.

You can even have a master business card designed for yourself and have a few photocopies run off onto an A4 sheet. Any good copying shop will have a paper guillotine that you can use to cut your cards to size. Additionally, you may want to attach your business card to the top of your letter. But doing this you give the person receiving your package something to pin on their notice board, put in their desk drawer or even better, into their wallet.

Before going to the last item, I know that some may view the above suggestions as *un* rock-'n-roll or maybe even unnecessary. Well, my answer to this is that the music industry like any other industry, is a business – and it has become even more so. Gone are the days when record companies would splash out huge advances on *chancy* acts. The business is controlled by accountants and they only take risks on people who they consider are serious and professional in what they do. So it stands to reason, if you take yourself seriously, then other people will take you seriously. If you take the time to look and be professional, then others will treat you professionally. And hypothetically, if a very rock-'n-roll band like 'Green Day' was looking for a new member and requested demo packages, which ones do you think they'd look at first – the tacky ones or the well presented professional looking ones? You know it makes sense!

Additional Stationery. If you're using good ole' *snail* mail (not eMail) to send off your DP's, then make sure you use sturdy envelopes as you want the contents to arrive intact. It also creates a better impression than a cheap battered one. I suggest using well padded envelopes, otherwise you run the risk of your disk arriving at its destination in pieces.

I always have the address typed onto a plain white label as I feel it displays a more professional approach. It's also advisable to have your address on the back of the envelope so that if, due to any number of reasons, your package cannot be delivered, it will be sent back to you and you can then redirect it to somewhere else.

to sum up

I believe that in the music business first impressions are all important and it's imperative to portray as professional an image as possible. Naturally, the most wonderful looking stationery and well recorded demos will do you little good, if you cannot deliver in the actual live performance department – but that's why you practice!!!

Lastly, make sure your DP is concise, easy to read and contains the best examples of who and what you have to offer.

GOOD LUCK

drumming and your health

This chapter deals with the various aspects of a drummer's well being in relation to their playing. Before I get into the more obvious areas of this subject I'll start off with the most basic preparation to easier playing – setting up your drums.

Being comfortable behind your drums is of paramount importance to playing at your best, whether performing or practicing. It still amazes me to hear how little regard some drummers give to this important area of drumming. They don't seem to realize that being incorrectly positioned behind their drums will work against them before they even play the first note. Therefore, taking the time to set up in a correct manner is the first step to achieving optimum performance.

starting with the basics

For most styles of contemporary music around 95% (or sometimes more) of drumming takes place between the hihat, snare and bass drum. It therefore makes sense to begin by positioning those into a comfortable position. But even more important and often overlooked is the drum stool (or drum throne).

Think about it, your playing emanates from you – not your drum set. Sure the drums and cymbals deliver the sound, but you are the vehicle to do this. And if you're not sitting comfortably, then you're going to be continually working against yourself. So before you start with the three main *playing* components, give due consideration to how you set your stool. The first thing is to establish the correct height for your frame (body). This is also dependent on what foot technique you currently employ. Gaining optimum foot technique is about balance and establishing correct pivot points in the hip, knee and ankle joints to allow maximum flow of energy. As a general rule, should you get the sensation of falling forward into the drum set, then you'll have positioned your stool too high for your personal height. Likewise, if your stool is too low then your knees will be higher than your hips which will cause you to use too much energy. This will make playing the pedals a tiresome job, because you'll have to virtually *lift* your legs to play the pedals – this of course applies to basic heel up technique. For both of the above situations your pivot points will be incorrect and if none of this makes any sense, seek out the advice of a good teacher to help you.

    On to the **snare drum**. As a general rule: ensure that the playing surface (the drumhead) is approximately belt height level. Generally, if the drum is too low then you may find a problem playing rim shots because the top of your thigh will get in the way of the stroke – the only way to get around this is to play in a French grip position – confused? Ask your teacher. Also, with a snare drum positioned too low, you expend unnecessary energy as your stick has more downward distance to travel before making contact with the drumhead as opposed to the shorter route by the drum being at the correct height. Then again, having your snare drum too high will force your arms to work more because you'll be playing with your arms in an unnatural higher position, all the time resulting in increased tension in the shoulders and neck. The general rule here is for your arms to have a 90-degree angle between the forearm (lower arm) and bicep (upper arm). This forms the principle for using Gladstone technique which is one of the most energy efficient ways to play. Again, if this sounds weird then ask your teacher or someone who specializes in Gladstone technique.

    You can however try this little test to get an idea of what I'm talking about here. Sitting where you are, place your hands on your thighs. Now focus on how your shoulders feel when your hands are resting. They should feel relaxed – right? Now raise your hands to chest height and extend them out in front of you for around half a minute. How do your shoulders feel now? Tense? Now lower your hands to where your forearms are parallel to the floor and where your upper arm is vertical to the floor. You should immediately feel a release of tension? Therefore, by having this

90-degree angle in the arms with your playing surface around belt height, there is minimum stress on the shoulders and arms, thereby encouraging optimum performance.

The tilt angle of your snare is a matter of personal choice depending on your playing style and the grip used. I personally have my snare tilted toward me as this reflects the grip I use and I find it easier to play rim shots. Also, the drum at this angle acts as a nice *springboard* onto the first tom in front of me. You can check out other drummers like Dom Famularo and Kenny Aronoff, who use the same technique as me, to get a better idea on this – or check me out on YouTube.

Bass drum and **hihat**. When positioning my bass drum and hihat, I make sure that I am not awkwardly twisting my upper body to the left or right when I place my feet on the pedals. A common fault is twisting to the left by placing the hihat too close to the body. This twisted position will, after a time, create lower back pain which everyone can do without. Also, be aware of how far you sit from the pedals. Sit too close and you'll feel cramped, unable to work freely and it will be virtually impossible to play foot strokes. Have the pedals too far forward where your ankles are way in front of your knees (looking from the top down again), and you'll have to virtually lift your legs to play heel up approach – however this position is good for heel down playing in using only foot strokes.

It's important to point out that the advice I'm offering here may confuse some and is not intended to be a lesson on technique. I am merely pointing out that certain positions work better with certain techniques. The aim here is for you to think about placement of your three main playing components, with the other equally important one being the drum throne. Thereafter, once you've got these into position where you feel comfortable, you can move on to the rest of your set-up.

add the toms, cymbals, cowbell and...

The choice is up to you whether you want to have toms mounted on the bass drum, on a rack, or tom clamps onto cymbals stands. I personally only use free standing bass drums because of the angle I have my bass pointing at, which is around the '2 o'clock' position. This means that if I mounted toms onto the bass drum then they would be too far to my left. Find what works best for you. The best advice I can give is to make sure that your toms are tightly positioned with no large gaps or angles, that they reflect the grip you use and that you can move comfortably around the kit without feeling restricted in any way.

The **ride cymbal** should be at a level and angle where you do not have to play with your arm raised too high or at too much of a side angle because this will tax the shoulder and quickly tire you out.

Your **crash cymbals** should be positioned within easy reach so as not to cause you to over extend and unbalance yourself when playing them. Also, the height that you have them will depend on your personal preferences and the music you play. I generally tend to have my cymbals around shoulder height or just above, so that I am not reaching to up too high to play them. I also make sure that I can touch each cymbal without over-extending myself in any way. This allows me to move around the kit fluidly, with minimum wasted energy.

A lot of drummers who play various styles may vary their set-up in raising the height of their cymbals when playing a louder (rock) gig, to allow for a punchier attack and approach. Then, when playing a softer (jazz) gig might use fewer cymbals which are then also in a lower position to accommodate the style of music and encourage playing easier.

By considering the above points you should be able to find a position that is comfortable and encourages easier playing. If you're fairly new to drumming then do bear in mind that as your technique develops, you will inevitably make changes to the way you currently position your set-up.

Remember also that the type of music you play will not only determine how you position your kit, but will also affect what size drums to use and the tuning of them. For example: Jazz drummers in general tune their drums higher than rock drummers. This is because jazz requires a tighter more controlled sound and this tone of the drums is more suited to the music style. Also, because the drumheads are tightly tuned, they enable the drummer to execute intricate patterns with the most economical amount of effort. This is especially relevant when using brushes as the same drummer would find playing the same patterns more tiring and difficult on a kit tuned looser for rock applications.

the 'shock effect'

Readers of the first edition of Rhythm of the Head have no doubt by now seen quite a few changes in some of the more

technical explanations I offer in this revised book. This is because some thirteen years have gone by since the first book and quite frankly, I am a much better drummer now and I have a greater knowledge of technique in general due to my extensive involvement in education. Wherever possible, I try to retain the original text and advice from the first edition. However, if there is something that I now do differently or more efficiently, then obviously I am very keen to impart this newer knowledge and advice. Little did I know thirteen years ago that the advice I'm about to offer leaned greatly toward Gladstone technique (also called the Free Stroke) which now forms the basis of my playing and what I teach. Live and learn as they say!

The following could do with an actual physical demonstration to more effectively put across what I want to communicate. Nevertheless, I've decided to include this advice not only to cause you to think about this area of your drumming, but perhaps to even discuss with your teacher (if you have one) or other drummers. Even some drummers with considerable experience may not be aware of what I'm about to share here.

The first few years of my drumming life wrecked havoc on my hands and wrists. The reason being that when hitting a drum I was not allowing the *shock* of the stick to disperse. This shock was even more apparent when playing rim shots. This may sound a bit strange as you may think that by releasing the stick you're likely to drop it. The following is the explanation from the original book:

"This release of the stick is really only a slight relaxing of the grip, a split second after impact. It is an action not clearly visible on casual observation, but more of the physical act and sensation by the drummer. What this does is save your hands and wrists so they aren't absorbing the shock of the strokes and as mentioned, will be extremely beneficial especially if you play hard rim shots a lot of the time. If you've been playing for a number of years and have stick breaking problems it may not be only due to playing hard, but may be from playing too stiff and not dissipating the shock of the stick effectively. I used to break a lot of sticks before I started using this method and can honestly say that at the most I've broken five sticks over the last 10 years! Nowadays my sticks tend to wear down in the middle where I pay rim shots and this is my reason for throwing them out".

Okay, here's the updated version: It's not really a relaxing of the grip, as the grip is relaxed all the time – which is the essence of Gladstone technique. The Gladstone technique encourages total free rebound, and the manner in which the fulcrum shifts and how the relaxed hand grip is employed allows this to happen. So while I am not going to go into a detailed explanation on Gladstone technique here, the common remaining factor here is to let the stick rebound freely off the head. This will save your hands, give you a bigger sound, save your heads, sticks and cymbals, and you will develop much better (natural) technical facility. If this intrigues you then hunt down a good teacher or drummer who really knows Gladstone technique and who can correctly impart this knowledge to you.

In regard to playing with chipped sticks, do bear in mind you run the risk of injuring yourself! If you've ever had the misfortune of catching a splinter from a chipped stick under a fingernail (ouch, ouch, ouch!) you'll know what I mean. If your sticks are chipped and you can't immediately afford new ones, then either tape them up, wear drummer's gloves or trim off the splintered bits – believe me, it's worth the effort.

Lastly, and still on the subject of sticks... I've had young students with small hands walk into my teaching studio and pull out a pair of tree trunks (2B weight sticks) and wonder why they can't play effectively. Use sticks that are right for the size of your hand and suit the application of the music you're playing. If you're playing heavy rock with a pair of 7A (jazz) sticks, then you may have a mismatch on your hands (sorry, couldn't resist the pun), and vice versa.

breathing

A common fault with a lot of drummers is storing tension in their neck and shoulders. This is often attributed to being nervous, but is also a result of holding their breath while playing. For example: when coming up to play a fast fill many drummers will hold their breath, raise and fill the shoulders with tension, which will of course inhibit natural flow. It's a bit like applying the brakes when trying to go faster. By consciously relaxing your neck and shoulders and keeping your arms in a natural playing position combined with natural breathing, the tension is taken out of this situation. It's a fact that all great players play in a relaxed manner to achieve a fluid and effortless result in the drumming. Here's a cool breathing exercise which is great for relieving tension...

Sit down on your drum stool and let your arms hang freely

by your side. Feel the sensation of your buttocks planted firmly on the stool, thereby establishing a solid center of gravity.

Bend forward so that your head goes down towards your drum kit. Now slowly come back, vertebra by vertebra, letting your head follow this action until you reach your original position. Your shoulders should now be naturally rounded. Close your eyes and breathe in through the nose with the mouth closed. Imagine breathing right down to into the abdomen and feel the abdomen expand as you breathe in counting slowly to six. When you reach six, hold the breath for another six counts and then slowly exhale and release the air through your mouth again to the count of six. Take a couple of normal breaths to make sure all the stale air is released then repeat the process. By doing this a few times you will feel well centered, void of any tension and ready to play.

If you're on stage feeling tense and unsettled, when there's a break in the music do as many sequences of this breathing exercise as you can manage (even one will help). If you don't want to attract any attention to yourself, then don't do the bending forward bit, only the breathing. Just don't get so carried away that you miss your cue and forget to come in with the rest of the band! They won't be amused – then again, maybe they will!

finding your center of balance

I have sometimes seen drummers rock from side to side while they play. This is due to having a bad center of balance on their stool. If you get the sensation of being unbalanced, especially when playing double bass pedals, then you may want to try the following exercise.

Sit on your drum stool away from the drum kit. Let you arms hang freely by your side. Play alternate eighth notes (RLRL etc) with your feet at about 80bpm. However, only <u>push up</u> your heels when playing these notes. Do this by using your lower leg muscles (calf and shin) to push up the heels. Don't lift from the thighs to raise the heels. While doing this concentrate on being firmly planted on your pivot point – your buttocks. Let the movement in your hips feel free. If the muscle toward the back of your thigh (joining onto the hip) feels tense, then you know you're not pushing up with the lower leg muscles, but lifting up from the thigh. This movement is what causes the unbalance.

When the floor exercise feels cool then move onto the pedals. Use a mirror to check for any side-to-side swaying movement. If there is excessive movement then go back to the floor exercise and maybe also slow the rhythm down until there is no upper body swaying. Once you're comfortable, progress from single notes to any variations between the feet, from doubles to paradiddles to triplets and so on. After enough practice at this you will cease swaying and be steadier on your seat.

get into shape for the music you play

Aside from an energetic singer who moves a lot on stage, drumming is the most physically demanding of all the instruments in a normal band set up. You're constantly on the move and if you're part of a very high energy level band then you know how physically draining this can be. So it's advisable to take the precaution of being in shape so that you can cope with the demands of whatever gig you're playing.

I don't believe in using any substances to increase my energy and help me cope with the demands of playing. I like to always have my own natural senses about me and know that I am personally responsible for anything good (or bad) happening in my playing. Anyway, the euphoria of playing good music and being pleased with my drumming is a natural enough high for me.

It's surprising how many drummers I meet are into martial arts in some form or another. I have involved myself in Tai Chi Chuan and also Karate, so would like to give you a word of caution about hard martial art styles such as Karate or Kung Fu. It can be dangerous and at times detrimental to your drumming. I fractured a little finger and thumb and sprained others while sparring. Carl Palmer stopped Karate after breaking a big toe. The positive side of doing a martial art is that while not directly aiding your drumming, helps to improve and centre your concentration. And Tai Chi in particular is great for improving balance and poise.

Another popular sport with drummers seems to be squash. Maybe it's the pleasure of knocking the hell out of things that turns us on – who knows? You have to be pretty weird to earn a living from banging away on a wooden or metal cylinder covered by a membrane!

Whatever sport or physical exercise you choose to keep in shape will be beneficial to your health and your drumming. Just do this in moderation and if it's a contact sport, then take care.

good food and good rest = good energy

Those of you who regularly undertake tours, or are away from home for extended periods will know how sensible eating helps to keep your energy levels up. Musicians are notorious for filling themselves up with junk food. So while getting real food is not always possible and I know that some of the time it's virtually impossible, taking meal supplements and vitamins is a good idea.

Getting enough sleep can sometimes also seem like a luxury. Just bear in mind that we function best after getting the right amount of rest and it makes good sense to sleep when you can. While on the subject of sleep, here is advice that is very close to my heart. If you're in a band where the band members share the driving (i.e. you don't have a dedicated driver), then a strong word of caution – **DON'T drive when you're tired**. While in the process of writing the first edition of this book I was involved in a pretty serious road accident while traveling with a band. The guy driving fell asleep at the wheel and we collided with two other vehicles that were (fortunately) parked at the time. Had someone been in the first car we hit, they would most certainly have been killed as we flattened it. Our tour bus was a complete write-off. We were all very fortunate and very lucky to come out of the accident with only some cuts, bruises, a few stitches and one broken hand (the driver's). It could have been a whole lot worse. So don't be stupid, if you're tired, pull up and rest, or let someone else take over the driving. If I've managed to scare or shock you with this story then I've succeeded in driving my message home.

guard those ears

Finally, a subject that concerns all musicians, not just us drummers – our hearing. When I was younger it was very uncool, so I foolishly thought, to use hearing protectors as it was considered very un rock-'n-roll. On reflection I wish I had been more un rock-'n-roll and protected my ears because I now have Tinnitus. For those of you who do not know what Tinnitus is, it's a continual noise in the ears. This noise can vary from a high-pitched ringing to a sound like water washing through your ears. One of the causes of Tinnitus is... you guessed it, loud noise. I can no longer lie in bed and enjoy complete silence, there is always ringing in my ears and to date there is no cure for it. Once you've got it – you've got it forever!

Have I scared you again? Good! Now buy some hearing protectors and look after your ears. Like your eyes they're the only set you'll ever get and once damaged, that's it! There are various types of ear protectors on the market from cheap disposable earplugs to sophisticated personalized attenuators that cut all the frequencies in a flat line. Make enquiries at your local music shop or ear specialist and safe guard your hearing. Remember that prevention is always better than cure.

to sum up

It is paramount to look after your health – without it you can't play the drums or live a normal life!

your personal global agency – the internet

We live in a very different world now, compared to the pre-internet one. You could say that the internet is as huge in creation and importance as the discovery of the wheel, the Law of gravity or electricity! It has revolutionized the world!

Whether you are an ardent online surfer or not, there is no way you can ignore the impact the world-wide-web has had – for better... or worse. The availability of information and resources that the web offers has certainly threatened many industries and even caused some to become extinct. One such industry that has certainly felt the impact of this is the recording industry. This has been both a good and bad thing; depending on which side of the fence you're sitting.

The record or CD sales industry has without a doubt taken a huge knock due to downloading and has changed how people now acquire music. Also, the iron fist clasp that record companies enjoyed over recording artists in the past has been dealt a considerable blow.

It is true that a multi-million dollar record deal may still be the dream and Holy Grail for most musicians. But the difference now is that artists have much more control over what they can or could accomplish. Many acts have signed record deals due to the success they have achieved as global internet artists. The British band The *Arctic Monkeys* is one such success story. They became one of the most downloaded bands on the net, which made record companies take note of this phenomenon and led to them signing a major deal.

These opportunities don't limit themselves only to bands. I have personally embraced the internet and used it to further my profile and career as a drummer in many ways. As proof, I encourage you to Google my name and see what comes up. You will see that aside from my official site www.georgvoros.com, I have a pretty healthy presence on the web. I appear on many sites around the world and have regularly seen my name pop up on music related sites, with no idea how it came to be there! And it doesn't matter how my name got there, the important thing is that it did. So how did I do this?

Well it started quite a few years back when I first saw the burgeoning power of the web, at a time when it wasn't even making that much of an impact. However, I was extremely curious to find out more about this thing but more importantly, what it was going to become. Was it a flash in the pan concept, or indeed what people were predicting it would become – a way of life? I invested in my first PC in 1998, which was quite late if you consider that Microsoft released the first commercial version of their Windows operating system in 1995 (Windows '95 anyone?). After some research, I decided to launch my website in 1998.

Having a personal website then was still a relatively new concept and did not immediately result in any great shakes or ground-breaking impact. But as time passed and the presence of the net grew (specifically after the year 2000), I discovered that I had an immensely powerful marketing tool at my fingertips. After 2000 everywhere you looked, you saw a *www* address. I now had a means of reaching people globally via this new, accepted medium of communication.

extending your reach

Around this time, I conducted a little experiment to see what might happen when marketing something via the web. I was curious to see what might be achieved if I wrote a few quirky songs and conjured up an offbeat image. Inspired by Sasha Baron's quirky TV character 'Ali G' and the 80's band 'Yello' whose music was mainly computer based, I called myself *Buzz*. Being pretty *old* in pop music terms (I was forty!), I disguised myself. I wore dark glasses, a funky hat, grew a cool goatee (and dyed it), designed a logo to portray this image and gave myself a period of six months to see what might result from this little escapade. I was pretty astonished at what happened...

Once I had written and recorded five songs, I sent out

around 40 to 60 eMails daily to publishing, management and record companies. Aside from a lot of the usual "thanks, but no thanks" replies, I received interest from a major record company and two management companies. One was interested in taking my music to Midem in Cannes, France – the annual International European trade show for all music genre professionals, providing business and networking markets. All this without even playing a solitary gig! Okay, okay, I know what you're thinking: "so what happened"? Well I didn't get signed to Chrysalis records (the major label) and my product didn't make it to Cannes. After some *to* and *fro-ing* the record company decided to 'pass' and the guy going to Cannes couldn't squeeze my product in as my material arrived too late for that to happen. But also, why nothing else happened was because I didn't put a band together to showcase the material live and didn't pursue the project. Again you ask "why"? Well, apart from my decision to make a major move in my life by relocating to another country, I found myself being pushed in different directions regarding my drumming career.

So, was I foolish in not following up on this project? Hey, to tell you the truth, I'll never know for sure, but the honest fact is that after the initial euphoria of the early interest shown, the project wasn't that precious to me, and it was almost enough for me to know that I could conjure up something like this and create notable interest out of nothing. So if I could achieve this, just think what <u>you</u> might accomplish if you put your mind, body and soul into a project that you truly believe in! Makes you think doesn't it? The evidence of an internet based project that I really was and am passionate about, and to which I've devoted a lot of time and effort is this book. And look where I managed to get it – my intended target audience – YOU!

a great marketing tool for drummers

The internet is an effective marketing tool to display your wares and showcase your talents via audio streaming or video on sites (such as YouTube), at little or no cost to you. My website has quite often functioned as an auditioning tool for me, thereby securing work for myself. I've sold my products over the net. My teaching practice has also been aided and built up via the information that is available 24/7 on my website.

However... and this is my disclaimer – all this happened because I could deliver the goods. Just remember that having the most amazing website will do you little good if you can't deliver the nitty gritty when required. Also, the information offered in this chapter is not intended to instruct you on how to turn yourself into an overnight success via the powerful marketing and sales options the internet offers. Rather, it is intended to serve as an enlightening vehicle to motivate you in taking the first steps to using the internet to further your career. And the advice about to follow can get you started in the right direction – if you haven't already done so.

promoting yourself on a networking site

For ease of explanation I am going to use MySpace as the sample site for information to be posted onto. However, what is mentioned here regarding MySpace pretty much covers what is needed for a personal site (that is if you are considering having one) or any other social networking website such as Facebook.

Lets first talk about your profile – in other words what goes onto your website and what is required. On MySpace you can have a professional looking site without a huge outlay. This can be accomplished using their free pre-made layouts. But what will really define the aesthetic appeal of your profile is not so much the background or the layout you choose, although this will make a difference, but rather what you actually put on your pages. The trend on MySpace has leaned heavily on filling up pages with a multitude of videos, slide shows and cheesy images. Most MySpace users do this simply because it's fun. Ultimately they don't care about analytics like traffic volume or click through rates. This means nothing to them. To most 'MySpacers' it's all about what happened on the weekend or what club everybody is going to after work on Friday. You, on the other hand will be out for something completely different...

If you would like to successfully use your MySpace page as a means to promote yourself or your band, then the worst thing you can do is take an unprofessional approach simply to try to fit in with other MySpacers. What you want instead is a profile that is clean, simple and inviting, which gets your message across in a concise and professional manner. That means no flash or glitter and only using one or two videos that really contribute to your web promotion agenda.

a new age

For a few years now, web design has been moving away

from the busy, loud-colored pages of the late 90's that were typically stuffed to the brim with animated GIFs and slow-loading background sounds. Nowadays, good web design is about flat, plain, simple, pages that load quickly.

So the bottom line is do you want to stand out from the crowd or just fit in with the rest? This will really define whether you have a truly professional layout, or ... just a waste of space. Once again this approach also applies to a personal website. It's your choice.

Some useful internet marketing tips

As you might expect, where there are millions of visitors daily, there are also a lot of failed marketing attempts. Here are some good tips for you to employ in order to maximize your internet marketing success:

Tip #1: **Create multiple profiles**. Sites like MySpace work through Attraction Marketing. Therefore, on social networking sites like these you need to make people find and like you. Depending on what you are portraying (promoting), you may want to consider creating multiple user profiles to increase the odds of being visited, rather than simply creating one, singular profile. Do a little research and see what works best for you. At present I prefer to have only one profile. But I know some drummers who have their personal profile, plus their bands profile, plus the bass player's and guitarist's profiles with links back to their site. This equals multiple sites all pointing towards one common denominator – you.

Tip #2: **Don't violate the user policies**. Don't spam! Spamming on any social networking site will get your profile deleted and a deleted profile doesn't generate anything. Most of all, spamming is annoying and will not win you any friends regardless of how stunning a site you may have created.

Tip #3: **Sell yourself first then your product**. What caused you to go out and buy a particular DVD or CD of a drummer or band? Because you *liked* them, that's why. You didn't buy the product first and then decide if you liked the artist (or not). No, you liked the artist or song first, which influenced your decision to buy the product. And let's face it, we all want people to buy what we're selling, so think along the same lines when marketing yourself.

You want to make as many of those 200-million plus internet users like you. When they become your cyber *friends*, then your marketing attempts from thereon will not be spam, but information they want. So make them like you first and then the *selling* can follow.

Tip #4: **Keep your pages slick**. Make your profile pages fun and cool, but above all else professional. Remember that the reason you're on the site is to spread awareness of you, your band, or your special thing – whatever that is. You are there to make cyber friends, but only as a means toward an end, and that is to raise your profile.

Another thing: keep your pages real. We know that the entertainment industry operates on a healthy dose of hype. So if you're stuck in one genre and can't play multiple musical styles, but are professing to be the next Josh Freese, then think again. Portray who you are truthfully. Just think of 'American Idol' and all those people who really *think* they can sing.

Tip #5: **Create blogs and videos about yourself.** Use a site like YouTube to promote yourself by uploading videos of your playing. Your aim here is for the masses of people out there to get to know about you and see what you do. This is an excellent medium to achieve this and costs zero. Start by logging onto YouTube and checking out the requirements for uploading. Just be honest with yourself and only offer the best representation of what you're about. The world is a big place and word spreads quickly – good or bad.

Create a blog and get people talking about you. Tell them about yourself and start the ball rolling. Once they get to know and trust you, you'll have an easier time converting them to your cause. That's the goal!

to sum up

Do you have what it takes to become internet famous? Musicians worldwide are frequent users of social networking sites. This type of networking allows them you to make a very personal connection with fans, which allows them to spread the word about their music. This social networking allows them the chance to get people to their shows which in turn creates awareness and who knows what possibilities for the future. You can do the same.

In this day and age the world is literally at your fingertips – the World Wide Web that is. Learn how to use your computer to raise awareness of who you are and what you have to offer. Join social networking sites and try to make as many cyber friends as possible. The main sites at the time of writing this book are MySpace, YouTube and Facebook – others are gaining ground fast. Build a website that suits your personality and update your pages on a regular basis. Otherwise people will just pass your site along if you can't keep their interest.

Lastly, believe in yourself and be yourself.

"Master the art of humbly saying, "I am" "I do" "I can" and following these up with truthful and convincing statements about yourself"
Georg Voros

creative visualization - a powerful process!

    I would like to begin this chapter by relating a story where I found myself struck down with a severe bout of flu. I rarely succumb to this kind of illness, but in this instance was laid flat for a full week and had to cancel all teaching, business and social engagements. As I lay in bed on the third day feeling sorry for myself, albeit with a clearer head, I recalled a conversation I had with a drummer when I was on the road doing some clinics. I had played some odd time signatures in my presentation that had prompted him to tell me about a weekend workshop he had attended hosted by the great Ephrain Toro. He mentioned a specific exercise that Ephrain presented that blew his mind. The exercise showed how Ephrain could play four different rhythms – all at the same time – in other words a different figure on each limb. I was intrigued when he told me this and vowed that I would try it someday as it sounded like something cool to master.

    Well… that day had arrived. With nothing better to do at the time, I decided that I would attempt this exercise – in my head at first. As I lay in bed, I closed my eyes and mentally pictured a square divided into four equal segments. The top left segment represented my left hand, the top right my right hand, the bottom left my left foot and finally the bottom right was for my right foot. To make this easier to understand, imagine watching a TV screen where the producer has divided the screen into four squares. In each one of those square blocks, he has focused on a separate limb. As a result, you can see all four limbs of the drummer as he plays and you can zone in and focus on the left foot or the right hand, or whichever limb you want to check out.

To start my visualization exercise I focused on the top left segment assigned for my left hand to play ¼ notes on snare drum. As I *saw* the ¼ notes being played, I also *heard* them in my head as each note played. Once this was comfortable I shifted my attention to the top right block and started to mentally picture straight ⅛ notes being played on floor tom. When I focused on this top right block (right hand), I was still aware that in the top left block my left hand was *playing* those ¼ notes on snare drum. I found that as I focused on a particular block I saw this almost *lighting up*, as a further means of concentration on that particular limb. I would shift my focus back and forth between the two blocks to check on the two hands. Once I could do this mentally with ease, I focused on the bottom right block that represented my right foot on bass drum. In this bottom right block I started to *play* ⅛ note triplets, while the other two limbs carried on playing ¼ notes and straight ⅛ notes. I repeated the process here in shifting focus between these three blocks to ensure that each one was *playing* its assigned pattern. Finally, I focused on the 4th block, being the bottom left which represented my left foot on hi hat. In this segment I started to *play* ¹⁄₁₆ notes. I stumbled a little at first, but eventually had all four playing these different figures at the same time. I used the ¼ note figure as the *glue* which kept it all together and which all the other figures played off. I was elated as I had managed to *play* this cool exercise in my head.

The next process was to attempt to allow my limbs to *feel* the exercise. I repeated the visualization and mentally allowed the limbs to enter the process by having them respond physically to the exercise. This resulted in the muscles twitching and flexing, just like they would react if I was physically playing my kit and sending down those mental messages into the four limbs.

The third and final process happened when I had recovered from the flu and couldn't wait to get into my studio to test out what I had done while I was in bed. I sat down at my drum set and started the process in the exact same sequence I had executed when playing in my mind – the left hand first, then the right, then the right foot and finally the left foot. Well guess what? I played it first time. I was amazed how it all clicked into place. I had cracked this really cool independence exercise because I had already played it in my mind.

The fact is that this process is really not that amazing and has been used throughout the ages. For example: When a pro golfer squares up to the ball and executes practice swings, what do you think he is doing? Well, he's practicing his perfect swing and *seeing* the ball fly through the air and fall exactly where he wants it to land. This kind of visualization practice has also been used in training by Olympic athletes, concert pianists preparing for a recital, architects who see the building in their mind first... and by drummers figuring out how to coordinate four limbs.

If you can clearly see, feel and hear a piece of music or pattern in your mind, then you will transfer this down to your limbs a lot easier. This does however take practice, but really does work. I often use this mental rehearsal and not only for drumming, but any other situation that requires focus on an end result.

left brain versus Right brain

It's an accepted fact and scientifically proven, that the left side of the brain is the reasoning or logical side, and the right side represents the creative or 'arty' side of our personalities. Mathematicians and accountants are predominantly left brain thinkers working with figures and traditionally find it difficult to think in pictures. Musicians or people involved in creative work operate predominantly with the right side of the brain and stink at logical or mundane jobs. These people also find it easier to imagine and form pictures in their mind, which is good news for you – the creative drummer!

I remember sitting in classrooms at school and often daydreaming. As an example I would *see* myself playing on stage with The Rolling Stones. This would seem so real that I could literally smell the air in the arena and feel the heat off the stage lights. Wonderful stuff! This didn't do my school marks any good but firmly confirmed that I was much more a right brain thinker than left. Over the years I've trained myself to bring the left brain more into play when carrying out repetitive tasks such as organizing myself administratively. Ugh! This doesn't happen naturally, but at least I can wrench myself into line to complete this activity efficiently when required.

how to get the visualization process started

If you have ever daydreamed then you already know what visualization is. However, the key is to be able to direct your imagination (visualization) and make it work for you. If you think these visualization processes sound daunting and have never

tried this before, then take heart and remember that just as with your drumming; the more you practice the better you will get.

Below are some pointers to get you started. You'll see that I've divided the visualization techniques into two separate areas. One is drum kit specific and the other a more general method. If you have never visualized before, then I suggest that you start with this first exercise.

1. General creative visualization

Step ONE is to fully relax. Sit or lie in a comfortable position, close your eyes and make a conscious effort to feel each part of your body relaxing. Start at your toes, and work all the way up to your head. As you do this, take slow, deep breaths. This should take a few minutes. Another term for this can be called meditation. (If you would like to learn more about this you can find many self-help books, CD's or mediation groups that teach you how to get more into meditation! For me there is nothing esoteric about meditation. It is quite simply, sitting or lying in a quiet place, consciously relaxing and clearing my mind of all busy thoughts and enjoying this peaceful time, however long or short).

Step TWO is to visualize. Many people can't *see* a mental picture at first – don't let this worry you. If you experience this, then I suggest that before you start the relaxation process outlined above, draw a simple object such as a square or triangle onto a piece of paper. Place the paper within easy reach and then start the relaxation exercise. When you have reached the point where you are fully relaxed, then open your eyes and focus on the object you have drawn on the paper. Take in the full image – the lines, the space between the lines... everything. Then close your eyes and try to hold that picture in your mind. Do this over and over until you can see the object.

Once you can comfortably do the paper exercise, then go onto more intricate objects such as focusing on your hand. You can also practice visualizing by picturing things you see and do in everyday life. Try to imagine enjoyable things such as your bedroom or eating your favorite meal. (These are the first two basic steps and these practice runs will help you *see* better, before trying your first real creative visualization).

Step THREE. When you are ready to do this then consider the following: Decide <u>what</u> it is that you want to work on. Pick your goal; maybe it's a simple groove or maybe a four-note coordination exercise. If this is the first time you are trying to do this, then I advise visualizing yourself playing something simple. As this becomes clearer you can move onto the more demanding stuff. It took me quite a while and lots of practice to *see*, *hear* and *feel* the more complex things I can now work on in my mind. Once again remember, the more you do this the better and easier it will become. Like any other learned skill.

Note: When closing their eyes, some people mistakenly expect to *see* something as clearly as when they have their eyes open. For me personally, when I see something in my mind, it is more like having awareness that there is an object I am looking at. Sometimes this can be crystal clear and at other times merely an outline or a *suggestion* that I am observing an object. I hope this helps in that you don't beat yourself up in not being able to see something as clearly as when you have your eyes open. This is where practice comes in.

2. Drum kit specific creative visualization

Sit down at your drums. Take some slow, deep breaths. Observe and enjoy the silence around you and relax. Let your arms hang loosely by your side and ensure that your shoulders are relaxed. Allow the drum throne to completely support your upper body. Let your legs and feet relax fully by consciously allowing your lower limbs to fully rest on the pedals. Check that your stomach and abdomen are also relaxed.

Now look at your drums and take in the full kit. Pay attention to detail. Observe every component individually at first, then collectively, so that you can see the full set in your peripheral vision. Peripheral vision means you do not have directed focus, but are taking in the general image of the whole picture. To help you understand this concept better, think of watching a movie, being aware of and taking in the whole scene, rather than focusing on something specific on the screen.

Now close your eyes, hold onto this picture, and attempt to see the full drum kit in your mind's eye. If at first you find this difficult to do then you're in good company as this is a learned skill and requires a bit of effort and patience to accomplish. Open your eyes again and repeat this exercise as many times as you need to form the picture of the full drum kit in your mind.

Once you are comfortable with this, close your eyes and see yourself playing whatever it is that you want to play – fully relaxed and exactly how you want that groove or pattern to be executed. If you do feel any tension or apprehension, then start again until you *feel* you are playing flawlessly. When you become adept at this exercise you should start to feel your muscles flex and flinch as you play in your mind. This means that the messages are being sent from your brain down to the limbs. When this happens you will also have reached the point when will be able to *hear* what you are playing in your mind.

Finally, pick up your drumsticks and now physically attempt to play what you have just played in your mind. If you falter, then go back and forth between mind-practice and physical-practice. The more you do this the easier and clearer it will become.

to sum up

If this all sounds a little *out there*, then take heart because it isn't. It is a very natural process that has been used throughout the centuries. As Peak Performance Expert, Researcher and Trainer Charles A. Garfield states: "I've discovered that numerous peak performers use the skill of mental rehearsal of visualization. They mentally run through important events before they happen".

I can without hesitation state that this kind of mental rehearsal definitely helps me achieve results quicker. I do this at home, in my studio, in bed before I go to sleep, when I wake up in the morning, on a plane, anywhere... the world is your rehearsal room so use it. Good luck!

don't hide your light under a drum set

The job of a drummer is to sit at the back and supply the beat for the musicians up front – right? Generally, this is the case as the drums are, in essence, an accompanying instrument. But this doesn't mean that you shouldn't explore and exploit other areas or hidden talents. Aside from taking the step to become a drummer and maybe even the band leader, maybe you have talents in other musical related areas. You might find that song writing is of real interest and comes easy to you, or maybe singing, or how about playing another instrument; you might even find that after a recording session you have a talent for production ...? Don't ignore any of these.

ignore discouragement

Often drummers aren't encouraged to explore other talents. One reason may be that the band considers the drummer to be just that – someone to *supply the beat* and nothing else. So encouragement for the drummer doesn't happen and as a result the additional talent that he or she may have is stifled. Sometimes drummers themselves may not openly admit to wanting to explore other avenues, possibly for fear of ridicule from their fellow musicians.

A good personal example of this goes back a number of years. A bunch of us musicians were standing around having a social drink and discussing music in general. We got on to the subject of our relative aims and goals for the future. Drummers spoke about doing 'drummy' type things, keyboard players aired their keyboard-related aspirations and so on. When it came to expressing my future goals, I said that I wanted to explore and expand on my singing. There were a few surprised looks and even a snigger from one of the other drummers present. Feeling a bit uncomfortable I nevertheless ignored this and carried on expressing my ideas outlining what I hoped to achieve.

A week or so later, the drummer who sneered at my singing aspirations came, probably out of curiosity, to the residency gig I was working with a top 40 band. In the band's repertoire I generally sang three to four songs a night. On spotting this drummer in the audience, I asked the band to make a change to our last set of the evening and play a song that featured me on lead vocal. I still remember the song – 'Right and wrong' by Joe Jackson. I sang the song; we played a few more and then finished for the evening. I walked off stage and headed for the dressing room when I noticed this drummer walking towards me. He sheepishly complimented me on my singing and how *surprised* he was that I could sing. Strangely enough, he wasn't sneering anymore. Need I say more?

do it!

When I first made some noises about writing this book, many people were surprised because to them I was Georg Voros the drummer, and nothing else. How was I going to write a book when I knew nothing about writing they asked? Well it's true, I didn't know a thing about writing, but I did know a lot about drums – and drumming was the subject I was going to write about. So, I made a start on the book and the more involved I became, the more I learned about writing. And the more I accomplished, the more I enjoyed the whole process. Additionally, as I wrote the content, I thought it might be a cool idea to include some sketches. Initially, I thought I'd have to employ the services of an artist, but then decided to have a go myself. Well, you've seen the results and while I don't profess to be a Picasso, I'm pretty pleased with my cartoon-like sketches – they get the message across. Did I think that I could do sketches before attempting them? The answer is no, but that didn't stop me trying.

It doesn't end there, as this book is self-published! What did I know about publishing six months prior to writing the first edition? Absolutely nothing! But now I know a great deal more and as you can see, it's all worked out pretty well and fallen nicely into place. At the time many doubted that I would accomplish

anything as their questioning comment was always, "what do you know about publishing"?

So over the years I've moved on from being known only as 'Georg Voros the drummer', to 'Georg Voros the author'. In fact, from the time the first edition of this book was published to this edition, I have involved myself in many additional areas of the business. Here they are:
- I have become a clinician
- I have raised my performance game many notches in having played at events with drummers like Marco Minnemann, Dom Famularo and Jojo Mayer.
- Together with my wife I founded South Africa's first and only magazine for drummers.
- I got into hosting drum events – big and small.
- I secured major gear endorsements.
- I write jingles for TV and radio.
- I have composed my own material and in 2009 am recording my first solo album, therefore moving into the 'artist' category too.
- I am an in-demand educator.

The object here is to not boast about my accomplishments, but to encourage you to think *outside of the box* – whether it is a box that you or others have placed you in. If you had said to me a few years ago that I might publish a drumming magazine, or share the stage with drummers like Dom or Marco, I might have thought you were out of your mind. But what happens is that one situation leads to another and it is possessing the mindset of being able to *dare yourself* to try something different, no matter what, that transports you *out of the box*, to achieve things which previously you may have thought were impossible.

Don't let anyone try and talk you out of, or put you off expanding your repertoire of talents. I'm sure Phil Collins is very pleased to have taken the leap from drummer to front man in Genesis, thereafter securing himself a phenomenally successful solo career. How about Dave Grohl? From achieving huge success with Nirvana as a drummer, he moved to the front of the stage with his band - The Foo Fighters. Then there's drummer Dave Clark? He formed 'The Dave Clark Five' in the 60's which went on to become an enormously successful act worldwide. Not only was he the bandleader, he handled the band's business affairs, wrote the material and if that wasn't enough, also sang lead vocals. At the time, many people said the band wouldn't amount to anything because it was unheard of to have a drummer as the *front man*. Well he sure proved them wrong didn't he? Oh, yes, I forgot to mention that the majority of the people who criticized him were other musicians – notably vocalists.

Hotel California is one of the classics from 'The Eagles' and features their ex-drummer Don Henley on lead vocals. He is another example of a singing drummer who went on to achieve incredible solo career success. Gino Vannelli is another ex-drummer with fantastic vocal ability who has enjoyed a huge solo career.

Then there are drummers who don't sing but play other instruments and write their own material. Jack de Johnette, aside from being an amazing drummer is also a master pianist. Dave Weckl plays piano, Joey Jordison plays guitar and Gary Husband has played piano with drumming legend Billy Cobham. I personally compose on this instrument.

to sum up

So, I reiterate, should you feel that you have a talent in another area of music, whether it be singing, playing another instrument, producing, arranging or whatever, <u>don't</u> let anyone tell you that you can't do it. Let your imagination run wild and prove them wrong. And even if what you attempt doesn't really come to much, you'll know you've given it your best shot, which is more than most are prepared to do.

But don't forget, the other side of the coin is that it could really work out and you could be leading your own band to success, developing a solo career, or turn into a hit producer...? All these things have happened to drummers who dared to dare.

I have this saying which I love to quote: "... *you'll never know if you don't try, and if you don't try you'll never know...*"

Good luck. Let me know how this book affects you by sending me an eMail via my website www.georgvoros.com. I look forward to hearing from you.

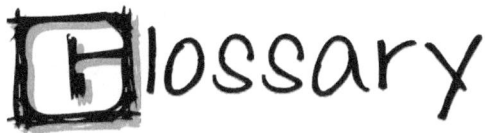

Glossary

The following is a list of terms and bywords that some readers may be unfamiliar with.

Accent	term given to strokes played with greater intensity – in other words, <u>louder</u>
Backbeat	these are the notes played on snare drum when laying down a groove – usually on beats 2 and 4
Beat	described in the dictionary as 'the basic rhythmic unit for a piece of music' – also used by drummers to describe a rhythm, as in a 'drum beat'
Click	the pulse laid down by an electronic rhythm device to which the drummer must play and keep time
Demo	a demonstration recording which can be used for promotional purposes
Double stroke roll	a rudiment consisting of 2 strokes played alternatively with each hand. RR LL RR LL etc
Dragging	the term applied when a drummer plays too much behind the beat and forces the temp to 'drag' – therefore slowing down the song
Drum machine	an electronic (digital) instrument into which rhythms can be programmed and then played back. Used for supplying a 'click' when writing music and also by drummers in practice situations
ff	Dynamic Marker - fortissimo, meaning louder than forte (which means loud) therefore VERY LOUD
Flam	a rudiment consisting of a soft (grace) note played just before the main principal note. The object being to 'thicken' the stroke
In the pocket	term applied when a drummer falls well into the groove with the other musicians whereby making it come 'alive' and creating the perfect groove. Also playing 'tight'
Loop	this term applies when a sequence of any number of bars programmed into a drum machine is made to repeat over and over and can only be halted by pressing the STOP button

Mallets	wooden (sometimes metal) sticks with rounded tips made from either felt, wood, rubber or yarn to play tuned percussion – they can also be used on drum kit to create different sounds
Metronome	a device – whether mechanical or digital – for beating out perfect time for musicians to play along with
Mix	this is the final stage of a recording session where the engineer balances all levels, tones and frequencies
Pitch	the word pitch is used to describe how high or low a note is. So in drumming it applies to how high or low the tuning of a drum is
Polyrhythm	the term applied when one rhythm has another counter rhythm played against it - ie. Three beats over two beats or four beats over three beats and so on.
pp	Dynamic Marker - pianissimo meaning very quiet
Realtime	the opposite to stepwrite. This is when the data to be entered into the drum machine is physically played in, like a 'real' drummer would
Rudiments	rudiments are sticking patterns and can also be considered to be the 'scales' of drumming. There are 26 standard rudiments and further extended rudiments. They are the building blocks for drumming
Session	term applied for a recording date in a studio
Set or setlist	term given for the order and arrangement of songs to be played in a performance – the repertoire
Stepwrite	the process whereby when programming a rhythm into a drum machine or sequencing program, the data is entered by gradually constructing a part via the machines programming functions
Tight	the term applied when a drummer is precise and crisp when laying down a groove – and doesn't sound like he is playing untidily by being 'loose' (similar to in the pocket)

Further recommended reading

The following list is not exhaustive and is merely a selection of books that I have used at some time in my drumming and teaching career.

Stick Control	George L Stone
Accents and Rebounds	George L Stone
The New Breed Volumes 1 and 2	Gary Chester
Advanced Funk Studies	Rick Latham
Advanced Techniques for the Modern Drummer	Jim Chapin
Snare Drum Rudiments	Buddy Rich
Applied Rhythms	Carl Palmer
When in Doubt Roll	Bill Bruford
New Directions in Rhythm	Joe Morello
Latin Grooves	Dave Hassell
Gene Krupa Drum Method *(my very first drum tutor book)*	Gene Krupa
The Art of Bop Drumming	John Riley
Odd Times	Rod Morgenstein
Sight Reading – The Rhythm Book	Alex Pertout
The Big Beat	Max Weinberg
'Traps' The Drum Wonder	Buddy Rich biography by Mel Torme
The Wrecking Crew	Hal Blaine biography
It's Your Move	Dom Famularo
The Cycle of Self Empowerment	Dom Famularo
Open Handed Playing	Claus Hessler & Dom Famularo
The Weaker Side	Dom Famularo & Stephane Chamberland
Afro Cuban Grooves for Bass and Drums	Robbie Ameen & Lincoln Goines
Eighth Note Rock	Glenn Ceglia
Rhythmic Perspectives	Gavin Harrison

Creating Performance Excellence

$21.95 for printed book.. ISBN 978-0-620-51491-0
$15.95 for eBook. ISBN 978-0-620-52340-0

This practically orientated and concise book by internationally renowned drummer, educator and author Georg Voros focuses on the essential tools required to develop the correct mind-set and methods, helping to ensure you deliver your best performance every time.
You will discover the refreshingly simple to apply 'RPD Process of Performance' which can greatly increase your understanding of how to effectively structure your preparation for any kind of performance or project.
This book is a must have for any performing artist - beginner to professional...

"I found this book to be an exceptional example of the wonders of realizing ones goals and ultimately, one more part of one's huge potential. It really tickled me in all the right places and having known and 'performed' with Georg over a number of years, I was not surprised by his excellent 'performance' in putting it so simply...down to earth and straight."
Greg Hadjiyorki Georgiades - MUSICIAN! BA(Psyc,Soc) Hons(Psyc) MA(Clin Psyc)

Fame Art Fortune

$21.95 for printed book. ISBN 978-0-620-51490-3
$15.95 for eBook. ISBN 978-0-620-52339-4

They don't teach this stuff in school!
This brand new book by Georg is based on his widely read first book 'Rhythm of the Head'. Originally written by a drummer for drummers, his first music orientated motivational book captured the imagination of drummers around the world, eventually being read by other instrumentalists and singers. Many commented how the philosophy of Rhythm of the Head applied to everyone, regardless of genre, age or instrument.
After many requests for Georg to release a more generalized book dealing with the valuable information covered in Rhythm of the Head, he literally
're-wrote' the book. The result is an easy to read, street-wise and motivational work which hits home and applies to any musician and performing artist.

"Mr Voros' book is full of common sense and wisdom, dispensed in a positive and practical manner. Inwardly digest"
- Bill Bruford (renowned drummer, composer and bandleader)

www.ingramcontent.com/pod-product-compliance
Lightning Source LLC
Chambersburg PA
CBHW021407290426
44108CB00010B/421